The Time-Optimized Life

The TIME-OPTIMIZED Life

Moving Everyday Preparation, Execution and Control from Finite to Infinite

DAVID BUCK WITH THE REV. DR. SUSAN ROSE

NEW YORK

LONDON • NASHVILLE • MELBOURNE • VANCOUVER

The Time-Optimized Life

Moving Everyday Preparation, Execution and Control from Finite to Infinite

Published in New York, New York, by Morgan James Publishing. Morgan James is a trademark of Morgan James, LLC. www.MorganJamesPublishing.com

Proudly distributed by Publishers Group West®

Scripture taken from THE HOLY BIBLE, NEW INTERNATIONAL VERSION ®. Copyright© 1973, 1978, 1984, 2011 by Biblica, Inc.™. Used by permission of Zondervan.

Morgan James BOGO™

A **FREE** ebook edition is available for you or a friend with the purchase of this print book.

CLEARLY SIGN YOUR NAME ABOVE

Instructions to claim your free ebook edition:
1. Visit MorganJamesBOGO.com
2. Sign your name CLEARLY in the space above
3. Complete the form and submit a photo of this entire page
4. You or your friend can download the ebook to your preferred device

ISBN 9781636982625 paperback
ISBN 9781636982632 ebook
Library of Congress Control Number:
2023942077

Cover & Interior Design by:
Christopher Kirk
www.GFSstudio.com

Morgan James PUBLISHING **Builds** *with...* **Habitat for Humanity** Peninsula and Greater Williamsburg

Morgan James is a proud partner of Habitat for Humanity Peninsula and Greater Williamsburg. Partners in building since 2006.

Get involved today! Visit: www.morgan-james-publishing.com/giving-back

To my parents, Ken and Karen Buck.
While living in eternity now, they taught me the value of time
through their love, wisdom, and guidance.

Table of Contents

Acknowledgments

As a Christian and person of faith, I need to give thanks to God. This book has been a journey, one that has taught me so much, including an understanding of how much more I need to learn. I firmly believe that comes from the Creator.

My wife, the Rev. Dr. Susan Rose (who you will learn about and meet in the book) has been supportive throughout our marriage. When it came time to start *The Time-Optimized Life*, I was lovingly encouraged.

My two children, Kenneth and Blake, are inspirations because they live their lives so differently than I did at their ages. They seek the right balance of adventure and responsibility. They want to time-optimize life now, finding worth in professional pursuits while not neglecting the personal experiences life offers. My sons have inspired me to evaluate and change my approach.

There are six people featured within these pages that exemplify time optimization. Matt Anselmo, Ellie Buck, Tracy Holmes Sr., Dr. Divya Jaitly, Rev. Dr. Hunter Camp, and Julie Blacutt gave of their time to share their personal strengths that will benefit you, the reader.

Through her attention to detail, my editor Cortney Donelson maintained my voice but made the book a cleaner read.

Finally, thank you to Morgan James Publishing—the entire team—as it takes many hands to send a book out to the world.

My time-optimized journey has taken decades (and will continue). Seeds of time management were planted early and throughout my career, then nurtured by incredible leaders and mentors who gave the right amount of guidance and direction. Karen Bartz, Bill Cagle, and Fred Ichniowski were there, and continue to be there today.

Before You Begin

Wait! Hang on a second!

Maybe you are reading this page because you are considering purchasing *The Time-Optimized Life*. You might have received the book as a gift. Perhaps you've started and stumbled onto this page on your way back to where you last stopped reading.

Whatever the circumstance, consider this before starting or going further in the book: *The Time-Optimized Life* was inspired by the Time Management Analysis (TMA). The TMA is a self-assessment tool that uses your responses to provide you with a detailed report on your abilities to plan, administer tasks, focus, organize, and take care of yourself.

While the book certainly stands on its own and will provide you with valuable advice, I want to provide you with the opportunity to personalize your experience with *The*

Time-Optimized Life. I am offering the occasion to take the TMA and get back the full report (a $39.00 value) for free as a *thank you* for having this book in your hands.

Here is the web address:

www.infinitylifestyledesign.com/tma-book

Simply provide your name, email, and then answer the twenty scenarios provided in the survey. A custom report will come to you within forty-eight hours. Keep it close as you progress through *The Time-Optimized Life.* Use it as a tool to gain greater control to help move your feeling of time from finite to infinite.

INTRODUCTION

The Spark for Time Optimization

T he spark for time optimization came out of the data compiled from two tools used at Kairos Management Solutions called the Retirement Time Analysis (RTA) and the Time Management Analysis (TMA).

To understand how to help someone with their time management, the TMA lists a series of scenarios, which the participant rates back to their comfort level or acumen to accomplish or execute. The situations created came from a review of dozens of articles, white papers, and books describing and explaining the best time management practices. The data was as wide as it was deep, with plenty of opinions and also much agreement on what it takes for a person to manage their time well.

The attributes were compiled, categorized, and merged to establish five priority categories of time management: planning, task management or execution, focus, organization, and personal care. Each category has sections within it to broaden the scope but still help define solid tactics to become proficient in a particular category.

The TMA provides a series of classifications that help show individuals where they are on their time management continuum. Using the acronym TIME, the assessment classifies a person either time Talented, Inclusive, Modest, or Expand. As I have worked with clients, trying to move them to a talented position, I found the approach needs to be a continuous one. There is no magic formula or quick way to use your time well. Therefore, "management" did not seem like it was enough. I have managed things in my life badly. *Optimize* better described the pathway needed for someone to be time talented and to stay there. Optimization is proactive; management can be reactive. Optimization lends itself to improvement; manage can sound like maintain.

I want to make sure you see your use of time as continuous improvement.

CHRONOS AND KAIROS

Everyone is a time manager. Everyone. Decisions—like getting up and walking to the kitchen to grab a bite to eat, spending thirty minutes to exercise, reading a book (this one, hopefully), looking for a new job, planning a wedding, attending church, or making a presentation—all require a use of time.

We measure time in so many ways. There are objective methods tied to specific segments like seconds, minutes, hours, days, months, years, and decades. We also provide arbitrary measures to our time. When some event or experience is enjoyable, we can proclaim the time went by quickly. Conversely, time can move slowly when it is an activity we do not like. Our perspective of time can be skewed, depending on the circumstances. In my native language of English, the definition of time flows back and forth between these two personal and dispassionate concepts that sometimes require further explanation or clarification. That is why I like the way time was approached in the language of the ancient Greeks. They used two words, *chronos* and *kairos*.

Chronos is the measurable, or quantitative, aspect of time. Look up and see what time it is on the clock right now. You are referencing chronos time. Required to attend a meeting for ninety minutes, you've just spent some chronos time. It is forward-moving time, defined and calculated. Chronos is the way we estimate our plans and quantify our performance.

Kairos is subjective but no less important to understand because it is qualitative. As a time manager (remember, we are all time managers), you will find the development of a program or strategy is kairos-based, while the execution is chronos-based. Instances of joy, frustration, satisfaction, determination, resolution, and completion can be tied to a set chronos measure but are more deeply expressed through a kairos explanation.

A couple of the best moments of time in my life were being present at each of the births of my two sons. From a chronos standpoint, I can tell you their birth dates and about the time each was born (I may need to ask my wife for clarification). These fixed occasions were (and still are) important to upcoming events in their lives. However, what makes the birthdays important days for me is found in the kairos element.

For Kenneth, it was his instant eye contact with me the moment I said, "Hey, bud." For Blake, it was the endless parade of nurses who came in to see the huge baby (he was born at ten pounds, ten ounces). There was also the joy of seeing Kenneth so excited to meet his new little brother. To only say the birth of a child happened at a particular date and time robs the experience of the kairos details, the precious periods of unmeasured time filled with the richness of life.

The challenge people have with their time management is a lack of balance or symmetry with chronos and kairos. Scheduling and programming are populated with too many activities, meetings, tasks and projects—so that chronos crowds out kairos, causing frustration because there is always something to do and not enough time to get it done. Conversely, a lack of structure and relying too much on kairos usually leads to missed deadlines and unmet expectations that trigger disappointment for ourselves and others.

After finishing *The Time-Optimized Life*, I want you to have chronos and kairos adaptability. By proactively *planning*, you will have a firm understanding of the chronos tools available to firm up how to prepare and track the use of your personal and professional time. Prioritizing the *tasks* to be completed and giving versatility to the ongoing list shall generate kairos opportunities. The ability to *focus* ought to strengthen chronos while initiating kairos. Seeing the need to be *organized* constructs chronos guardrails of kairos circumstances. Finally, allocating formal chronos periods of *personal care* apportions kairos periods of physical and mental health.

By reading this book, I am asking you to invest in chronos to get kairos. Our time in life is finite; it is fixed. The mission of Kairos Management solutions and

The Time-Optimized Life is to help you move time (chronos and kairos) from finite to infinite by optimizing your time management.

THE REALITY CHECK

About five times a week, my wife Susan and I walk three to four miles in the early mornings. It is time we purposely invest in personal care, but also in each other. We reminisce and reflect, talk about our children, discuss current events, and confer on our work. However, we also plan and strategize. We look forward to spending both chronos and kairos time together. As a natural extension, many a morning has been devoted to the topic of this book.

As I put shape and form around the outline I had created, Susan was there to provide valuable insights and perspective. You will find out throughout this book that we approach the idea of time management differently. My wife is a voracious reader and a curious learner. She is constantly challenging herself to improve in a variety of areas. This led her to achieve her doctorate in ministry.

In Susan's pursuit of continuing education, she has run across some blind spots in the practical application of self-help or support books. Authors tend to provide themselves as an example to emulate, which may not align with the environment of the reader. Therefore, on one of our morning walks, as I was explaining a part of the book I was working on, she asked, "Can I write a chapter?"

Because I admire and respect her insights, it was a no-brainer for me. For much of this book, you will hear me, my perspective, and my methods. However, it will also be filled with reality checks of additional views from people I know and respect. The culmination will occur with Susan's take on time management, which will help you determine what reality looks like and to emphasize the importance of establishing a time-optimized life that is *your life.*

ASK YOURSELF, "WHY?"

I am hopeful this book is in your hand (or on your screen) because you want to read it and not because you must read it. Either way, I want you to come away with the sense that preemptively managing your time is an opening to experience more that life has to offer. In reading through the material, constantly ask yourself, "Why is living a time-optimized life important to me?"

You'll find the answer will be different based on the circumstance, but the question will help you maintain a mindset that balances the chronos (quantitative) and kairos (qualitative) elements of time usage.

CHAPTER I

What Is Time Optimization?

And God said, "Let there be lights in the vault of the sky to separate the day from the night, and let them serve as signs to mark sacred times, and days and years."
(Genesis 1:14)

I dreaded presentation review day. I had recently been promoted to a strategic selling role that required a lot of planning. So I created detailed reports to make the case for the products and desired actions I wanted the client to take. Prior to any business meeting with a major customer, I had the "meeting before the meeting" with my boss.

It could be outright painful. On occasion, we were stuck on one slide for thirty minutes. My supervisor would contest me on the slightest data point and take me down rabbit holes I felt were irrelevant.

However, what I considered a waste of time ended up being a time saver. By being grilled and challenged prior to the client meeting, I went into it confident and prepared. Some of the crazy scenarios my boss would concoct to test my knowledge and comfort level came up from time to time while I was presenting in front of the customer.

What I did not realize . . . my time was being optimized. Because my boss invested time at the front end, I was prepared for the meeting. I would execute smoothly, showing the materials well. As a result, I had better control to achieve the outcomes I needed. I was being time-optimized before I even knew it.

THE VIEW OF TIME

The very concept of time runs the gambit. From simple declarative statements like, "I am running late!" to scientific expositions in Stephen Hawking's best-selling book *The Brief History of Time*, time is thought of in both elementary and complex terms.

It is easy to assume all humans look at time the same, but we don't. There are over forty different types of calendars used throughout the world. The ones employed by most of humanity can be narrowed to a number between seven and nine.[1]

We are separated by time zones that may change over the course of the year. Do you want to talk to someone in India and you are in the United States? You better account for the time shift of plus or minus thirty minutes. Any consumer-based products company working with suppliers in China plan their production and distribution around the Chinese New Year.

Our worldview, cultural norms, religious perspectives (or lack thereof), family, and choice of friends are just a sample of external influences that shape our internal perspective of time. Because religion plays an important role in all our lives, even if we do not practice one, let's review that a bit.

CHRISTIANITY

I lead with Christianity because it is my religion and the one most familiar to how I live my life. Given the monotheistic nature of Christianity, existence (and time itself) has a defined beginning when God made the universe. We humans, created by God, live in a temporal or earthy reality for a period and then, upon our death, move to an eternal existence.[2]

The concept of time in eternity is a subject of much discussion and argument. I am not going to get into that here. However, when looking at the temporal aspect, Christians have one life viewed from the lens of a linear experience, interrupted by a passing away, then move to a new perpetual actuality.

JUDAISM

Being the forerunner to Christianity and Islam, Judaism in some sense, sets the time foundation for the other two. While there is much debate within the Jewish community of time in relation to their faith and tradition, there is a sense and curiosity of time before the formation of the known universe.[3] Where Christians and Muslims tend to focus on life after death, the Jewish person tends to reflect on time as a form of creation and G-d's continuing role in that.

ISLAM

Like Judaism and Christianity, time in the known universe has a foundation set and given by God. However, of the major monotheistic religions, Islam seems to place a higher emphasis on time as a resource—using it wisely and being mindful of wasting moments.[4] The personal actions of the individual and the time they spend play an enormous role in how God will favor them in the life to come.

HINDUISM

To my Western upbringing, the concept of time in Hinduism is quite different. From Hindu observations of the world around them or of natural law, the existence of a person is bound by two suppositions. The first is that everything that is born dies. The second is that everything that then dies is created in another form.[5] The universe and time are inextricably linked with no notion of a beginning or first creation. Time is cyclical, like a plant that begins from a seed, grows to produce its own seed, and dies to leave the seed to start the series again.

BUDDHISM

To a committed Buddhist, this book might be irrelevant. Like all religions where there are many schools of thought, the same applies to Buddhism. But there appears to be a consensus that time is an illusion.[6] The linear nature of time (past, present, and future) is a construct. Humans aspire to be liberated from suffering to bliss or tranquility. Being synchronized with time, even the measurement and passing of it, is less important and less significant to life.

NATURALISM

While there are wide philosophical views within Naturalism—and even of its definition—a broad description is one where the word *super* is removed from the supernatural, and the pursuit of truth is found in the sciences and natural processes. Add in time and you can get a timeless naturalism (eternalism) and temporal naturalism (presentism).[7] In each case, time is invested to understand certainty, fact, and accuracy.

The table below nicely summaries these worldviews regarding time and their impacts on humanity.

Worldview	Function of Time	Human Impact of Time
Christianity	Linear	Birth, death, resurrection
Judaism	Linear	Birth, death, afterlife
Islam	Linear	Birth, death, paradise
Hinduism	Cyclical	Succession of birth, death, birth
Buddhism	Illusionary	Path of the liberation from suffering
Naturalism	Varied	Birth, death, end of existence

FIGURE 1:1 WORLDVIEWS OF TIME

So how does this apply to time management? Look at it as perspective and approach. Depending on the seriousness of a person's worldview, that can have a significant impact on the attitude to manage and oversee the use of time. If you see your reality as cyclical, time management could have a heavy emphasis on education and process understanding. If time is more imaginary or ethereal, concentration may well be placed in moment-by-moment emphasis. Contingent on the rigidness of your linear perspective, time can be populated by a series of intentional events meant to achieve certain outcomes. When life is only defined by what is known of natural processes, time management may have a narrow objective.

Because each person comes to the approach and use of time differently, expansive applications of time management could easily cause uncommon applications in order to maximize the use of time. Therefore, it is important to establish a definition that allows for common guidelines and indicators for consistent understanding.

THE DEFINITION OF TIME MANAGEMENT

American Founding Father Benjamin Franklin spoke a lot about time management and the efficient use of time. Number six of his established thirteen virtues states, "Lose no time; be always employed in something useful; cut off all unnecessary actions."[8] In addition, as noted in *Poor Richard's Almanack, 1746*, Franklin declares, "Dost thou love life? Then do not squander Time; for that's the Stuff Life is made of."[9]

According to the career site Glassdoor, time management can be a beneficial discussion during a job interview. Their team states, "Time management is the ability to effectively prioritize your work. It's essentially your aptitude for staying productive and ensuring you are meeting your overall objectives."[10]

A time management leader from India, Brigadier Sushil Bhasin, declares in his book, *Million Dollar Second*, "If you are used to attacking mountains of accumulated work without a plan or strategy, prioritization is something easier said than done. It is a simple idea that calls for complex implementation process, which further calls for self-training and self-discipline."[11]

One of the most personally challenging volumes for me on productivity (because it requires a disciplined mindset) is Cal Newport's book, *Deep Work*. While not necessarily a definition, here is a time management call to action.

> *It's difficult to prevent the trivial from creeping into every corner of your schedule if you don't face, without flinching, your current balance between deep and shallow work, and then adopt the habit of pausing before action and asking, "What makes sense right now?" It's an idea that might sound extreme at first but will soon prove indispensable in your quest to take full advantage of the value of deep work:* Schedule every minute of your day[12]

There are so many other great examples and explanations of time and our ability to regulate it. Various ones relate back to the fixed value of time, say 86,400 seconds in a day, and emphasize the commonality we have to that set number. Others seek to break the length into smaller segments of planning. Still more highlight what happens when time is squandered, never to be reclaimed again.

Interestingly, as you review time management definitions (even the ones noted above), they tie in foundations of the "function of time" noted in Figure 1:1.

An approach or solution to a time management problem can be linear. Problem identified, problem worked, problem solved. It can require a cyclical attitude. Problem identified, problem worked, problem adjusted, problem worked, problem adjusted, problem solved. Time may well be employed as illusionary, looking backward and wondering if there could have been a better way. Problem analyzed, problem reviewed, problem learned. Whatever your worldview, there is a time management definition to help tie back to your circumstance.

In 2021, during the height of COVID-19, I engaged in a process to quantify and measure how people manage their time. Sure, there are numerous tracking tools and manual ways to apply time "used to produce or be productive." When launching the Time Management Analysis (TMA) tool, I soon found some interesting trends. People identified with time management and perceived good versus bad use of time but had difficulty with the proper treatment of their time. Through hundreds of TMA assessments completed, analyzed, examined, and studied, the definition of time management has been refined, sharpened, and simplified to provide a nucleus of actionable parameters. The definition tied to the subject matter in this book is as follows:

"Time Management is the right preparation, along with the right execution, to control productivity."

In effect, the key words to remember (and that will be mentioned over and over) are preparation, execution, and control (PEC). Each one of these in itself requires an expense of time to manage time better.

To help put this into perspective, think about the time you have had to assemble something you have never done before, using a set of instructions (or not). In the course of my life, I have done this dozens of times. Things like bicycles, outdoor play sets, toys, bookshelves, desks, other furniture, trade show exhibits, and retail merchandise displays. My wife can attest to the many moments of "weeping and gnashing of teeth" as I struggled my way through the time management mess I put myself into. Reflecting back, when there were difficulties, I neglected one or more of the preparation, execution, or control principles. So, when navigating any action tied to your formal time management, weave in PEC.

PREPARATION

Preparation establishes the provision, design, forethought, and groundwork of time tied to a future project, task, event, or undertaking. When it came to children's toys and office furniture, I always spent more time when I dove right in and started the assembly instead of reading the instructions, ensuring I had all the parts, organizing the space, and checking to make sure I had all the right tools.

EXECUTION

After the plan is generated, time management then shifts to execution. It is as much procedure as it is technique. Once I have everything set to build the new desk, I scuttle any time efficiency if I had rather chosen to throw away the directions out of a false sense of confidence. Sure, I thought it would save time by not reading the instructions, but I ended up wasting far more time trying to figure out what parts to use in what areas.

CONTROL

An often-overlooked aspect, but just as important an element of time management, is control. *Your control.* The best preparation and execution can be nullified if you lack the authority over the period allocated for performance. In most scenarios, parents (at least in my case) would not attempt to put a new children's play set together in the dark, with children running around. I wanted to pick times when I could be focused and not distracted, interrupted, or have to say "no" every five seconds.

The next time you purchase an item with "some assembly required," know you are headed down a time management tunnel. That construction will be a combination of choices you choose to make and don't make, that will dictate the outcome based on how you integrate preparation, execution, and control. Lack of one or more, and (speaking from experience) you will suffer from time exasperation.

PEC can have a loose triune relationship (see Figure 1:2). Each one may be done well alone, but when aligned as a time management plan, the three can be executed as one. If you fail to plan well, it makes it difficult to execute, leaving command of the activity or task much more challenging. Instituting weak practices negates any well-established blueprint, curbing the influence of the use of time. Ignoring structure and constraints (control) after a good plan and process has been made will set you up for time chaos. Activities frequently require adjustments to the PEC triad time management definition. Knowing you have the flexibility to adjust one—or all—grafts PEC into a powerful methodology.

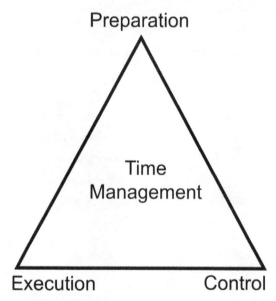

FIGURE 1:2 THE TRIUNE NATURE OF TIME MANAGEMENT

Now that time management is defined with its simplest form coming down to an easy acronym of PEC (preparation, execution, and control), where does this optimization stuff fit in? Well, I am glad I asked that question for you. Time management is not enough unless you introduce constant improvement to PEC whenever possible. That is *time-optimized time management*.

THE DEFINITION OF TIME-OPTIMIZED TIME MANAGEMENT

I worked for a company that integrated the principles of lean manufacturing into their production processes. *Lean* was created by Toyota to eliminate waste and inefficiency in its manufacturing operations.[13] Being in sales, I was not asked to be a subject matter expert, but I was encouraged to understand a broad outline because of the benefits it would provide when presenting the product to prospective and existing clients.

The five principles of lean are to identify value, map the value stream, create flow, establish pull, and seek perfection.[14] Treated not as a "one and done" tactic, the approach to lean is one of continuity and a forever pursuit of improvement. Perfection in step five is sought but never really obtained, which leads you back to step one to see where upgrades can take place. The time-optimized process borrows some elements from lean and adds to the definition of time management.

> "*Time-optimized time management* is a continuous pursuit of the right preparation, along with the right execution, to escalate broad control over personal productivity."

Instead of PEC being looked at as a onetime event, it is permanent and intensified, with the goal of getting you more time efficiency or yield and free up additional time to pursue other personal and professional interests. Sounds like the search for kairos time, doesn't it?

Like in lean manufacturing, the collective preparation, execution, and control become a tool to create time flow and establish pull to reduce time waste. The net result of time optimization is its own form of a search for perfection and that is to make the time you spend feel less finite and more infinite.

(PERPETUAL) PREPARATION

Elevating preparation from an isolated episode requires a look backward. While each project or pursuit will not have the same requirements, there is knowledge in preceding assignments. Time-optimized preparation taps into the previous knowledge and applying it in the present to help accomplish what needs to be done in the future. This type of preparation never ends; it is linear in execution and cyclical in evaluation.

(ESTABLISHED) EXECUTION

The police are established to protect society, keep order, enforce the law, and assist the citizens. The equivalent attitude needs to apply to your time-management process. The execution of a time-management plan needs to protect the time intended to be used. The process is there to keep order in the tactics. Procedures are in place to enforce structure and good time behavior. Finally, without any methods in place, you are not helping yourself or anyone else. In fact, you might be causing more harm than good. Execution here is a reaction to preparation. While linear in nature, you may find the execution sending you back to the preparation stage for modification.

(CORRECTED) CONTROL

You own your time. Sure, others impact, affect, and sway what you can and can't do. However, it is important to assume the responsibility of your time and be a steward of its use. That means getting proactive and not reactive. So many people struggle with time management because they do not like to say no, disappoint others, look selfish, seem distant, or come across as not caring. Control here does not deny assistance to others but provides your time more on your terms. That is where the correction or adjustment gets instituted. Corrected control is getting back on track, or diverting from preparation and/or execution to keep an original timeline.

FIGURE I:3 TIME OPTIMIZED TIME MANAGEMENT

Figure 1:3 brings in a deeper connection and relationship with PEC. Not like a relay race—where batons are passed from one runner to another—time-optimized preparation, execution, and control is deeper than cyclical and broader than linear. Time-heightened development allows for a change in direction while time continues to move forward, going "backward" to refine plans and processes to move "forward" in better control of the outcome. The PEC relationship plays itself out in dual micro and macro circumstances.

EXAMPLES OF TIME OPTIMIZATION

I have introduced this concept of time optimization, and it is "time" you saw some examples to bring context. In each scenario, you are introduced to a general time application or approach to typical events in a day. That example is then viewed through the lens of a time-optimization attitude, where you will see the situation and consequences will be much different.

General time application: Scheduling a meeting for Wednesday at 2 p.m., inviting the right people, and creating the topic and agenda.

Time optimization: Ask, "Do I really need to call a meeting?" If yes, develop the topic, goals, and content. Decide your to-dos before, during, and after the event. Establish an agenda tied to accomplishing your objectives. Determine who really needs to participate and only invite them. Conduct the meeting, staying on topic and on goal. Decide on any follow-up measures and ensure anyone impacted understands their role. Send a post-meeting communication, highlighting the key takeaways and remind any participants of assigned tasks.

General time application: Setting a task list, knowing what tasks need to be completed today, and reserving time to work on them.

Time optimization: Regulating a task system that allows for prioritizing, based on the level of importance and what truly needs to be done that day. Reserving time at the beginning of the day to verify the most important tasks are highlighted first and that they will be targeted for work and effort during the most productive time of the day. Being disciplined enough to stay on the most difficult and significant responsibilities and get those done. Work the secondary and lower-level ones at other times in the day when opportunities are created. Allocating time at the end of the day, reviewing the progress and status, seeing the needs for the next day, carrying-over any unfinished tasks, integrating them into the next day's list, and re-prioritizing.

General time application: Exercise set for thirty minutes on Monday, Wednesday, and Friday at 5:30 p.m.

Time optimization: In consultation with your doctor (or another appropriate professional), determine the best workout strategy based on your current health. Formalize the times on a calendar. Design a program with measurable goals. Record and track the days you exercise and note the progress you are making. When you have achieved necessary milestones, adjust the plans accordingly.

These three typical examples have certain commonalities. The "general time application" approach is somewhat vague, lacking one or more foundations of PEC. This is the attitude of so many in the way they look at points in life. For them, time management is a series of scheduled events or planned activities they will get to at some point. *Time optimization* puts in the structure of preparation, execution, and control, all the while integrating a continuousness and flexibility, but with firm intention, to regulate the outcome.

CHAPTER 2

The Five Areas of Optimization

Suppose one of you wants to build a tower. Won't you first sit down and
estimate the cost to see if you have enough money to complete it?
(Luke 14:28)

wo titans of modern business are Jeff Bezos and Elon Musk. The former for
founding the ecommerce giant Amazon, and the latter for Tesla, SpaceX, and
Twitter. Each billionaire built something out of nothing and has impacted
the lives of millions of people.

Amazon has created many *time-optimized* moments for me. I can make
enhanced and better-informed product decisions. Through free shipping with my
Prime membership, I have time choices. Do I want to travel directly to a retail
store and buy the product immediately? Can I wait twenty-four to forty-eight
hours for it to arrive on my doorstep?

While I do not own a Tesla, when I drive, I see them all over town. Tesla cars and solar panels are helping to mainstream the use of electric vehicles and reframing the approach of the automotive and energy industries. In addition, Musk's continued push for innovation and scientific advancement has helped maintain and even revive the US space program.

DIFFERENT BUT PRODUCTIVE APPROACHES

Bezos and Musk are two highly productive people. They represent examples of time-industrious managers. However, they have distinct differences in their approaches. As each assumed greater responsibilities and the nature of their roles changed, they enhanced and adapted their use of time to the changing priorities tied to their growing businesses.

Jeff Bezos rises at 6:30 a.m. every morning. He has set and predetermined activities before he dives into the workday. Time is invested in having coffee, reading the newspaper, eating a big breakfast (which he usually prepares for the entire family), and completing any personal chores. Bezos does this to help maintain not a work-life balance, but a work-life harmony.[1]

After attending to the personal aspects of his life, it is off to work. The business mogul prioritizes his day, allocating time for the most important decision-making when his brain is at its peak. "His approach is to make a few high-quality decisions per day instead of hundreds of low-quality decisions providing lackluster outcomes."[2] Therefore, as the day goes on, the priorities on the list become more secondary. It does not mean the ecommerce pioneer is not having an impact. He can take comfort in that vital, central, and key judgments are complete. The back half of the day is not a waste (think kairos or qualitative); in fact, it can still be productive. Bezos has just chosen high-optimum yield times.

The Amazon founder ends his formal business day at 5 p.m. But productivity does not stop. He has identified a second potential peak productivity time around and during dinner.[3] However, he is a stickler for getting enough sleep and is usually in bed early, normally getting eight hours.

Elon Musk is more like the Energizer Bunny with the slogan, "He keeps going and going and going." The head of SpaceX consumes time like a rocket expends fuel. "There's no denying that Musk's workaholic habits have had a huge impact on the world and yielded tremendous results."[4] He is known to put in between eighty and one hundred hours a week.

Musk begins at 7:00 a.m. (close to Bezos). Interestingly, he makes it a point to shower every day. Why is that meaningful? "Apart from the personal hygiene aspect, it's a proven fact that showers have several health benefits, including rejuvenation, washing away toxins, decreasing stress, improving immunity and blood circulation to name a few."[5] The engineer will also find inspiration while cleaning up.

Unlike his billionaire counterpart, Musk does not place much emphasis on eating. It is necessary, but he does not concern himself with what he consumes, indulging only at dinnertime. Furthermore, his workday will last until 1 a.m. He is committed to six or six-and-a-half hours of sleep, but from shower time onward, he is at it, full speed.

Variety is built into Musk's schedule, with no two days being the same. He is a big proponent of multitasking (we'll be spending a lot of time on this in the book, so hang on; I have some additional thoughts to share).[6] Elon is a focused business owner, spending upward of 80 percent of his time on his strength: engineering. To do this, the multiple-industry leader creates protected time and limits his access during certain periods of the day. Musk controls distractions and regulates interruptions. A continuous learner, he loves to read and constantly spends time in books and periodicals.

Being close to what drives efficiency, engagement, adeptness, and knowhow, the future-minded mega capitalist spends time on location, at his offices or in the factories. As a leader, this gives him the understanding to gauge the pulse of productivity and time skill at all levels of the organization.

Two men, who started small and now dominate their particular areas (with a little crossover, only between SpaceX and Blue Origin), have time management figured out, but it was a process. Jeff Bezos spent countless hours perfecting his fulfillment model. Elon Musk needed to figure out where best to allocate his efforts. I would bet that they are still amending and reworking set routines.

Your time-management journey will also change. Today, you may need to make a lot of smaller tactical decisions, knowing it will shift as your career adjusts. A productivity zone for you could be in the afternoon and not the morning. Eight hours of sleep in a busy life in the present feels more like a dream (pun intended) than any type of reality. Whatever the circumstances that make up life and time today, not having a system to meet and adapt to your wants will limit the means and potential of time optimization. While there is no need to follow the Bezos or Musk models (though each has aspects to emulate), there is a need for you to locate and instigate your standards. You can start through the five priority categories of time optimization: planning, task management, focus, organization, and personal care.

After comparing the two billionaires, I would evaluate their priority categories as such:

Ultra Billionaire	Planning	Task Management	Focus	Organization	Personal Care
Jeff Bezos	Day mapped out well	Prioritizes based on importance	Establishes productivity zones	Place boundaries on decision-making times	Solid sleep plan, starts with solid meal
Elon Musk	Sets a full schedule	Works the hours to complete necessary items	Determines zones of protection and limits interruptions	Develops and sets multiple strategic plans	Marginal sleep plan, does not eat three meals a day

FIGURE 2:1 BEZOS AND MUSK TIME MANAGEMENT SUMMARY

The rest of this chapter gives an overview of the classifications. You will find that you do some well and others not so well. Each category is not an all-or-nothing type. There are also sections in each group. Items will come to the surface that need your attention. Time optimization is a journey. In each opportunity you identify, preparation, execution, and control (PEC) need to be employed.

You will also want to ascertain if there is a linear (onetime), cyclical (keep coming back until it is right), or varied approach.

PLANNING

Pre-planning prevents poor performance.
Prior planning prevents poor performance.
Prior proper planning prevents poor performance.

I have heard many variations of the sentence known as the 4Ps, 5Ps, 6Ps, on up to even 12Ps of success. The most common term used—"Proper planning prevents poor performance"—is credited to James Baker, the former secretary of State of the United States.[7] That makes sense because I kept hearing it when I worked in retail management in the late 1980s and early '90s. Planning was always fundamental. Plans might need to be adjusted, but there was always an established proposal.

Planning is listed first because it is a foundation upon which all other time management actions happen or don't happen. The Bible has a great illustration of this in Luke 14:28–30.

> *Suppose one of you wants to build a tower. Won't you first sit down and estimate the cost to see if you have enough money to complete it? For if you lay the foundation and are not able to finish it, everyone who sees it will ridicule you, saying, "This person began to build and wasn't able to finish."*[8]

First, there is an idea to build something. The next step asks a question: "Won't you?" I love how this is phrased because it gives the context that sometimes "we don't" and, thus, set ourselves up to squander time. The planning occurs in earnest, and time is invested to answer the key goal of, "Do I have the funds to build the structure?" Whether you answer yes or no, it is not a waste of time. It brings clarity to the next steps. This is the essence of the "right preparation" in our time optimization definition. Before any construction begins, a period or periods of formulating and devising occur before the "right execution" is even considered. To begin to build and not finish is ridicule in the above passage; for us it is a major case of discarded time.

The word *planning* is broad and can cover a host of different aspects. Planning is a time-optimized attitude that spotlights five topics: setting personal goals, mapping ahead, being on-time for meetings, preparing as well as participating for and in meetings, and committing to completing assignments. These address business and our private, personal, and professional lives.

PERSONAL GOALS

Establishing personal goals are broader than private and should include business metrics that are tied directly to what you hope to accomplish in your career. That may seem like talking out of both sides of your mouth, but there is good reasoning for the blending.

A clear individual goal could be, "I want to run in a marathon." Using PEC, the time-optimized way, would be to develop practices and techniques to train in the proper way to run the necessary distance. To just jump out there on the day of the race would be a waste of time and a possible detriment to your health.

A potential personal business goal is to be promoted at work to, say, a sales director (sorry—being in sales for my career, I am partial there). To accomplish this goal, there needs to be a plan to perform well at work, to be considered (professional), and to determine what additional skills, experience, and education you must complete to have a shot at any future openings (personal). Walking into work and declaring yourself a leader is not a plan I would consider time-optimized.

MAPPING AHEAD

Before the age of smartphones, Google, or iPhone maps, and even Garmins, I was a traveling salesperson. I had a defined territory of stores I needed to visit at specific locations. Not having the luxury of plugging in addresses and letting a program chart my drive, I used a paper map. In my company car was a stack of city and state street maps with highlighted areas representing my customers. Before I began my work week, I found the appropriate diagram, plotted out which stores and in what order I would stop, based on what needed to be accomplished. To just get up, get in the car, and start driving would accomplish burning a lot of gas and putting unneeded miles on the vehicle.

We spent time in Chapter 1 looking at concepts of time and whether we are fixed on linear or cyclical. Mapping ahead actually does both. The future is defined by looking forward and understanding the places you need to go. However, you can and should look at the past to help shape the way you decide to map ahead.

Mapping ahead takes work and activity of the present and projects outcomes into the future. It is an investment now to help reduce ineffective time that may come. It is a habit of reviewing the now and figuring out the when so that everything is not needed immediately or directly.

MEETINGS

For much of my career, I have worked remotely, outside of a structured headquarters and inside a home office. In that time, particularly being involved in sales, I was insulated from meeting fatigue and frustration. It was not until I was back in a formal business office, did I see what a time-drain meetings can be to any best laid plans.

Time optimization looks at meetings as opportunities. On the front end, the desire is to push and challenge (being mindful of the facilitator and audience) by asking, "Should the meeting even take place?" Knowing the purpose up front might bring resolution outside a formal gathering.

If the encounter must take place, then there must be a commitment to making the most of the time. As the organizer, an investment must be made before the event to establish an agenda (including goals), which is communicated prior to the occasion. Leadership is shown by being there and starting the meeting on time. The plan should be to seek engagement and contribution from all participants. Before adjourning, a clear follow-up plan (with responsibilities) must be articulated. That action plan must be re-communicated in a summary as soon as possible after the closing of the meeting.

As a participant, you owe it to the organizer to review any materials beforehand. Honor the commitment, show up on time, and be ready to take part. When it comes time to wrap up, clearly determine if your assistance is needed for post-meeting follow-up and give clear assurance you understand. Affirm any communication for follow-up that comes from the meeting coordinator.

COMPLETING ASSIGNMENTS

When I would become frustrated by others not getting back to me, a former boss and still mentor of mine would say, "You gotta follow up on people's follow-up." That was his signal to me to plan on always being ready to track to-dos, but also to look at yourself to see if there was anything you left out there that was unclear, preventing others from following up with you.

Completing assignments is and should be about honoring obligations to yourself and to others. Nothing more can set a chain of time-management blunders than not committing and seeing the item through until the end . . . on time. More of a behavior than a system, finishing what you start is intertwined with so many other time-management advice in this book—and is a huge component of control in PEC.

The planning processes for a couple of the richest people on the planet are robust and vigorous.

Back in 2017, Elon Musk did the ultimate planning exercise and developed a list of everything he says he will accomplish by 2030.

> *To say that billionaire tech-preneur Elon Musk is a busy man would be an understatement. Musk finds himself at the helm of a number of companies, each of which have goals firmly set on the future.*
>
> *To bring electric autonomous vehicles (EAVs) and renewable energy solutions forward, he has Tesla. To give humankind a chance at becoming a multi-planetary species, there's SpaceX. To transform transportation—and build better tunnels—he's working with the Boring Company. To have a hand at the conscientious development of artificial intelligence (AI), he's involved with OpenAI. And, lastly, to augment the human brain's capabilities, he's put up Neuralink.*[9]

In 2018, Bezos was direct about his approach to mapping ahead.

> *Amazon CEO Jeff Bezos says he "very rarely" focuses on the short-term, daily operations of Amazon, and instead is looking and working years ahead. Bezos discussed his management style, and explained how he and his leadership prefer to focus on the long-term goals at Amazon. He said he pretty much only works on Amazon's roadmap, and leaves daily tasks to other Amazon employees.*[10]

In the coming pages, time-optimized planning will help you look well into the future, without missing the opportunities of the present.

TASK MANAGEMENT

I had a nickname from some of my direct reports. I was called the *Task Master*. Depending on the day and situation, that might have been a term of endearment or of frustration. In the early stages of Microsoft Outlook, I embraced its task function and dove into creating, adjusting, forwarding, and completing them. What I liked about the process was not having to write forwarded tasks over and over again, like you still have to do with a paper planner. I could be reminded through notifications and pop-ups when something was due. I could tie it back to emails and ensure I responded to important communications. I was in full PEC mode before preparation, execution, and control were even conceived and united.

HAVING A LIST

Managing tasks has come a long way. There are so many examples to track your assignments and to-dos. Between Outlook, Google, Apple, apps, online calendars and planners—this should be an easy add and routine procedure in any time-optimization process. However, coming out of the COVID-19 pandemic, I looked at the participants in the Time Management Analysis assessment and only 38 percent maintained a task list consistently. There is no lane to optimization if establishing, adjusting, and keeping an assignment record are not in the mix. In a couple of chapters, we will cover this in detail.

PRIORITIZATION

Another aspect of task administration that happens quite frequently is the "all are equal" philosophy. A typical way is to line up all the tasks for the day and start at the top of the list, or even worse, get the easy ones done first. At the end of the duration, all the second-tier activities are done, and the most important are still left. What happens next is a scramble to shift the remaining tasks to tomorrow, realizing the important ones are really important now. However, old habits die hard, and subsequently, the same thing happens on the succeeding day.

MULTITASKING

No task discussion would be complete without the concept of multitasking. I have some firm ideas and concepts around multitasking that many would dispute (though I do have a lot of research from much smarter people than me to back me up). I am going to wait until you make your way there in the fourth chapter to get into details.

I will put this teaser out there: I can agree that a musician who plays an instrument and is able to sing at the same time can be a plausible example of multitasking. To get to that level requires hours and hours of practice. Time is invested in learning to just play the instrument. More time is invested in learning just to sing. At some point, even more time is spent trying to do both at the same time, at a quality level that does not leave cats and dogs running for cover.

Now, if you are willing to invest the hours necessary to check your email on your laptop while in your manager's weekly staff meeting, being fully engaged in each activity without missing anything, have at it. I would suggest you invest the effort in time optimization and not test the patience of the boss.

Getting back to our billionaires, take a look at how each manages his tasks.

For Musk:

One thing is to create a task list for every single day, and the other one is to carry it out. Elon Musk does it by dividing the day [into 5-minute slots.] Then he thinks about how much time he needs to carry out each task. Once he figure[s] this out, he then assign[s] tasks to time slots in his calendar. It is merging your to-do list for the day with your calendar.[11]

For Bezos:

Whether working on a complex project or even a small set of tasks, it's extremely important to define the scope. Doing so, as Bezos explained in a past letter to shareholders, requires first recognizing what a "good" result looks like. Then, you must understand and have realistic expectations for how much work it will take to achieve that result.[12]

They have a clear and defined list, prioritized to concentrate on the importance of each one, and they direct their efforts one at a time.

FOCUS

When I established the priority categories in the Time Management Analysis (TMA) and began to receive assessments back, I soon found out that *focus* was (and continues to be) the biggest time management challenge for the average person. Part of the issue is that some of the types within focused time are hard to quantify and measure. Focus can be a battle of willpower, which many lose, only to find themselves having to restructure and adapt to adjusted deadlines and needs. In the time-optimization dance of preparation, execution, and control, focus is all about control. Time-optimized focus has six areas with external and internal components, which is why we'll spend two chapters in the book on this topic.

PROCRASTINATION

As I mentioned, focus is the premier time-management obstacle for people, and procrastination is the prevalent impediment to being focused. Postponement of tasks or activities starts at the beginning or the preparation of PEC. A six-word DIY project like, "Paint the inside of the house," seems direct and to the point. However, the sheer scope of the undertaking can make it easy to delay. To advance forward, it is best to break the plan into smaller, incremental steps that allow you to feel good about the accomplishment.

- ✓ Get supplies
- ✓ Prep bedroom
- ✓ Paint bedroom
- ✓ Check supplies
- ✓ Prep bathroom
- ✓ Paint bathroom

When a delay occurs, a backlog of time happens, continuing to build until things stop getting done. We'll be taking a step-by-step look at this later in the book.

MOTIVATION

Do you know people in your life who always seem to have a positive outlook on everything? Maybe you are that person. I am not. As I get older, I understand there are times when I allow myself to be annoyed or bothered, and I am fully embracing that I can be a cranky old fart. At least I do recognize it.

However, having the right motivation in time-optimized focus is a gift that everyone can have with practice and consistency. Focused motivation is not an unrealistic pursuit to overlook anything that could negatively impact what you are doing. It is an attitude that you will be inspired to control (in PEC) events and circumstances to achieve the desired time-managed outcome.

You are allowed to be cantankerous, but that must be recognized and overcome to set back in the motivated attitude that will allow you to finish.

DISTRACTIONS

I can get easily distracted. It is my biggest time management challenge, and I fall into temptation too many times.

When my dad was trying to quit smoking, he took up exercising to help improve his health. He told me one day about the frustration he was having with stopping the cigarette habit. After working out, he would put his regular clothes back on and smell the residual smoke odor. It became more pronounced when he got in the car to drive home. Instead of it being a reminder to quit, it was a trigger for him to smoke. He would be driving down the road, not even realizing he had finished half a cigarette. I totally appreciate what he went through because I experience the same thing with my smartphone. I battle checking it when a notification comes in and find myself with the phone in my hand before even realizing it is there. I must take concrete steps to not fall into temptation, usually by leaving the device in a different room.

Distractions are considered an internal trial to overcome. Sure, there may be some outside influences, but the choice to limit them falls back on you (and me with my phone, in particular). Time distraction occurs in three major domains. The first is all the electronics we have around us and the apps or tools tied to them. The second is personal, bound to how well we take care of ourselves by what we choose to keep around our work area. The third are professional distractions. These are different than interruptions, which we will discuss in a second. Professional distractions are those work-related, environment-associated, and activity-driven times we choose to stop what we are doing to address and engage in the disturbance.

Distractions are dangerous because it is easy to lose time and not realize what has been wasted until it's too late. Overcome your internal time obstacles and you find PEC working together so much better.

TALKING

Yogi Berra was a successful baseball manager who was just about as famous for his one-line quotes. When it comes to talking, he said, "It was impossible to get a conversation going, everybody was talking too much."[13]

Discussions certainly should happen in the preparation and execution areas of PEC. Deliberation when laying the groundwork of a task or project is time-optimized thinking. Consultation during the implementation phase brings clarity and moves the system along. When P and E stall because of too much gabbing, it is time to reinsert C into the mix.

There are many ways to talk less and get control back. However, there should be an investment of time to understand the nature of why you (or others) continue to talk instead of act. Swiftly instituting control without context may affect E (execution), giving the false sense that the P (preparation) was inadequate. In the external aspect of focus in Chapter 6, we will study talking and its impact on time optimization.

INTERRUPTIONS

Earlier in the chapter, I mentioned that for a large part of my career, I worked remotely and did not have to deal with the dynamics of day-to-day office interactions. After enjoying that position for quite some time, I was promoted into a situation where I oversaw a new major client for my employer. One of the stipulations was that I was given an "office" in their corporate headquarters, to be readily accessible for my contacts there. I put *office* in quotes because the space could not hold two chairs. Anytime someone from my employer came to visit me, they had to sit in the aisle for there to be room to talk. While I could have used this example up in the distraction section, it was the interruptions that caused me the most headaches. Sitting in my micro-cubicle, surrounded by other vendors in the same situation, a parade of client employees wanting me to stop what I was doing and address their concerns constantly halted my momentum. It was hard to manage my time.

The opposite of distractions, interruptions are *external* intrusions that are generally out of your control (until you apply time-optimized techniques; more to come). Someone has a need they must fulfill, and you are deemed the right person to help them do that.

Also, like distractions, we will explore three categories of interruptions and the actions you can take to hold them down and control time to optimize your productivity.

While this is a section discussing the concept of *focus*, the first challenge with interruptions is a lack of planning. When someone comes a knockin' at your door, saying, "Hey, can I have a second?" if you have not set-up the day and cannot demonstrate what you need to get done, you have no data to explain why now is not a good time.

The second option is to be aware of your surroundings. Proactively investing time to understand when and where interruptions may come (particularly when there are high-priority items to complete) helps you anticipate and plan for different actions.

Then the third consideration is the ways incoming communications break through your ability to focus and concentrate. Cut them (where possible), and productivity awaits.

The PEC of time optimization fits right into battling interruptions. Prepare for them, execute your plan when stopped, and control the circumstances because of your proactive nature.

SAYING NO

No is a powerful word. Children get frustrated because they hear no a lot from their mother and/or father. Many parents learn to say no frequently with their kids (at least that was the case with mine). That changes when it comes to friends and can be difficult at work.

The time-optimized approach to declining requests or demands of your time is not rudely cutting someone else off. It goes back to integrating PEC, so the solution becomes "No, but . . ."

"I am unable right now, but [*insert preparation*]. It will take an hour because of [*insert execution*]. We will start tomorrow at 2 p.m. and be done in ninety minutes [*establishing control*]."

"I am already on three committees; I just don't have the time. However, have you considered these people *[preparation]*? I can help contact them to see if they are interested *[execution]*. Give me until next Tuesday, and I will get back to you *[control]*."

There will be instances of directly and emphatically delivering a hard no, and every person should practice and be ready to say it. Though, in most cases, a refusal, coupled with a desire to see if it is worth your time to accommodate, sets seeds of future time-optimization that may ultimately lead to "yes" for you and the other party.

It's been a while since we discussed the gazillionaires. Getting to their level of success requires a constant emphasis on their vision or convictions.

In the case of Jeff Bezos, he credits his success with Amazon to the purchaser. "Watch any video of Bezos talking about business, or Amazon's growth, or his own life lessons, and within seconds he will inevitably talk customer-centricity."[14] Bezos made his focus on the customer, and that was and has been the driving force for his company.

For the CEO of SpaceX and Tesla, focus is improvement. "'Focus on signal over noise. Don't waste time on stuff that doesn't actually make things better,' he says. For Musk the 'signal' is product development, to which he dedicates the majority of his attention . . ."[15] That is also a great mission statement for life.

ORGANIZATION

I write this section with hesitation because I am going to enter spouse disclosure territory.

Susan (my wife) and I approach organization very differently. We each have offices in our home, and they are right next to each other. On any given day, if you stand at the doorway and look into my office, there is little clutter. My workspace is clear. The books are organized, and the paperwork is filed. Anything that is not needed is either hung up or put away. From a visual scan, it is arranged.

Take six steps to the left, and you'll enter my wife's office. The shelves are overflowing with books. Her extra chair is filled with items to be mailed, folders, and even a sweater she wears when she is cold. Move your eyes to her desk, and she has two stacks of paper, about a dozen books, notepads, and what seems like endless written Post-it notes everywhere. She has totes containing a host of old papers and writings stacked up on an adjacent wall. To my eyes, it always looks a little chaotic.

At this point, some of you think I am crazy and are wondering if I am still married. The answer is yes; keep reading.

While I prefer for everyone to have a neat and unadorned workspace, I have also come to realize that time-optimized organization goes much deeper than the surface, and here is the premise: If Susan was standing in our kitchen and you were in her office, and you shouted out to her, "Where is *such and such* paperwork?" She would immediately answer something like, "Go to the second stack of papers—closest to the computer—and about halfway in, you will see a blue folder. Look under that, and you will find it." Guess what? It will be there.

Now, if you do the same with me, I will probably answer, "Check my filing cabinet and look under the 'home improvement' file folder, and it should be there." After a few minutes, you will ask, "I checked there and don't see it; where else could you have put it?"

My response might be, "Oh sorry, try the 'other expenses' folder." In a short time, you may come back with, "I did not see it there, either." To which I will come in, look in the file cabinet myself and say, "Oh yeah, sorry again, that is in the 'to be filed' area I have in the holder on the side of the cabinet."

In each case, the item was found, but which one took the least amount of time and effort? I'll let you answer that out loud yourself, and that should confirm to you that I am still married.

Other than surface-level set-up and configurations, time-optimized organization sees broader patterns in actions and activities. In Chapter 7, we will dive into the importance of finishing what you start, using a calendar, and having a general sense of organization. Like the previous materials already introduced, we will see how PEC weaves itself throughout.

FINISHING

For those of you paying attention, you might be asking, "Hey, didn't this dude talk about completing assignments back under planning? What is the difference?" Good for you! Yes, there is a difference, and if you need to go back and review, not a problem—I will wait.

Welcome back.

Completing Assignments back in the *Planning* category is tied to meeting an obligation to you or to others and is tied to a specific pursuit or endeavor. *Finishing* what you start in the *Organization* category is ongoing and mindset-driven. As activities are completed, there is less to juggle or rearrange. It is an attitude set well for PEC. You constantly *prepare* to always *execute* and *control* the outcome. That's proactive organization.

CALENDAR

I could write an entire book on calendar management. Your calendar is the single most important and powerful time management tool. It leans heavily on the preparation, triggers execution, and must be used to control time. The calendar is utilized in all five priority categories (Planning, Tasks, Focus, Organization, and Personal Care). If you lack a consistent and detailed calendar strategy, my advice is to start there with your time optimization design (which will be discussed in Chapter 10), after you are done reading this book.

ORGANIZED

My introduction to *organization* lays out the essence of general time-optimized organization. Again, while I encourage "space and place" thinking, the ultimate aim here is to find what you need as quickly as possible. However, what is not noted in my previous marital confession, it is necessary that a certain level of your orderliness plan must have an element of access understanding from anyone. This is very important in an office or business setting. So much time gets wasted in companies with employee turnover because effort is expended just to find something of a former employee.

For Elon Musk to maintain his hectic schedule, there must be an arrangement or method he has established. "People would be impressed when they hear that he is able to allocate time for himself, his hobbies, and his family while working 11–14 hours a day and sleeping 6 hours. He explains that Timeboxing is the secret behind his day-to-day accomplishments."[16] Timeboxing is a methodical system (using a calendar) to align tasks and schedules to provide bursts of productivity.

"So Bezos has a system to organize his time. 'I try to organize my personal time so that I live mostly about 2 to 3 years out . . .'"[17] For him, organizing is a long-term process.

Time optimization can handle the multiple-year strategy or the five-minute allocation of timeboxing.

PERSONAL CARE

If you have done any search of me on the internet, you know I am not a doctor. I have no formal medical training. I am not a nutritionist. What I am is a sixty-year-old man, who walks around twenty miles a week, tries to squeeze in a couple of exercise sessions as well, eats well enough (consumes way too much chocolate, though), has a beer most evenings, does not smoke, gave up soda in lieu of carbonated water, and I am at about the right weight for my age and body type.

This book is not an exercise program, weight loss resource, body cleansing, or nutrition plan manual. If you ask me for my advice, I will recommend you talk with your primary doctor about the best way you can care for yourself.

What the *Personal Care* section will cover are a few areas to help you *time optimize your time management.* While this will be the shortest chapter in the book, don't discount its impact on your ability to be productive. The more you take care of yourself, the better you can function in the four other categories.

SLEEP

Set the book down and plug "How much sleep do I need?" into your browser. Save a little time; don't worry about the correct capitalization and punctuation. Like me, you probably saw headings showing between seven to nine hours. For time optimization, I landed in the middle and chose eight hours. When you get to the chapter, I will back that up with a lot of supporting data. Remember, Bezos gets eight, and Musk gets six.

BREAKS

Staying in one spot and going on and on with a specific activity can lead to a diminished marginal return. That's a fancy economics term for not being as productive as when you started. Stepping away for a short period and not working (I know, counter-intuitive) helps reset the brain to come back and enhance your output.

EXERCISE

For so many of us, our business "work" in reality (with some irony) means we are mostly sedentary. We stay for long periods of time in one place—in a defined and confined area where we interact with our coworkers. Then, our personal lives are very busy with time-sensitive activities, having us moving but not in a formal or structured way. That is why some form of planned and scheduled exercise that raises your heart rate in some way gives your body (and mind) the energy to time optimize well.

SPIRITUALITY

I have gone back and forth about discussing the impact of spirituality on time optimization in this book. My faith plays a large role in my life and one I strive to be an even bigger impact with each passing year. I realize the pursuit of religion and one's belief system can be subjective and personal. However, I am going to include the subject. It will not be in the vein of proselytizing to my particular Christian worldview but to explore the time benefits of "a person's experience of, or a belief in, a power apart from his or her own existence."[20]

Investing time in pursuits that broaden thinking, challenge norms, enlighten the soul, and open the mind to new ways of reasoning is time well spent. Therefore, I want to include a section and be mindful to tie it back to time optimization and honor the command given in Scripture for someone of my faith to, "But in your hearts revere Christ as Lord. Always be prepared to give an answer to everyone who asks you to give the reason for the hope that you have. But do this with gentleness and respect . . ." (1 Peter 3:15–16).[21]

We spent time at the beginning of this chapter talking about the two rich and successful business guys and how they plan their days. We noted that Bezos commits to sleeping eight hours a night. "The revolutionary Bezos is a fitness enthusiast, and at the age of fifty-eight, he is fit, muscular, and healthy."[18]

It appears Musk has a different take. "Surprisingly, Musk has admitted (more than once!) that he wishes he could do without exercise. But of course, he still does [exercise]. In addition to 'lifting some weights' on his own, he also dabbles in Taekwondo, karate, judo, and Brazilian jiu-jitsu."[19]

THE REST OF THE JOURNEY

Bezos and Musk will be the last two "famous" people I feature. While I can't guarantee quotes or references from names you will recognize, the showcased personalities in the subsequent chapters are talented in a particular priority category (planning, tasks, focus, organization, and personal care). They are individuals I know well and care about. I am confident they will be inspirational to you because they have shown me through their actions and example, they get the concept of time optimization.

You'll also see us return again and again to our definition. "*Time-optimized* time management is a continuous pursuit of the right **preparation**, along with the right **execution**, to escalate broad **control** over personal productivity." **PEC** is an acronym that can be applied to any of the priority categories and the individual sections within.

As reviewed in Chapter 1, the worldview application of time (cyclical, linear, illusionary) will be referenced occasionally to add perspective around a particular element or point.

After navigating your way through the first nine chapters, number Ten helps you plan out your time-optimized approach. I do not expect nor recommend you adopt the Bezos or Musk models. I have used these successful business leaders throughout the second chapter to provide context and thoughts for consideration, not for them to show you the way. There are strengths and weaknesses in both, but you need to create what is right for your current situation and adapt as your life changes.

You've invested your time this far. Let's get into the time details.

CHAPTER 3

Time-Optimized Planning

We put up vision boards on mirrors or on the wall, things we imagine or want to have. We look at this and meditate on these every single day.
(Tracy Holmes)

I had a running joke with my mom up to my college years. In school, I was a pretty good student. I got *As* and *Bs*, showed up to class, did my homework, and turned in my assignments on time. I even graduated in the top ten of my class in high school. My parents never really bugged me about my schoolwork because I never really gave them an issue to be worried.

However, I had a bad habit of "waiting until the last minute" to complete my coursework. A teacher would give out an assignment that was due in two weeks. I would delay or ignore the effort that needed to be done. The night before the due date, my mother would see me working away as she headed to bed. Then would come the questions.

She would usually lead off with, "What are you working on?"

"Ah, I have a paper due in American History," I would respond.

Then came, "When is it due?"

Short answer, "In the morning."

Now fully into the routine, she would sigh. "And you are waiting until the night before to get it done?" A statement asked as a question.

Then with a smirk and well-rehearsed response, I would pause for dramatic effect and utter, "You know, Mom, I do my best work under pressure."

To which she would smile and shake her head. "You know, that may not work too well when you go to college."

Now would be my turn to sigh and say, "Yeah, yeah, you say that every time, but I always manage to get it done. It will be no different this time and when I go away."

She would give me the drawn-out and lengthened motherly, "Allllllrrrrrriiiiiii-ight," followed by, "Goodnight."

My mom was such a prophet of common sense. When I went away to the university, working under pressure was a horrible approach to a successful college career. Gone were the easy assignments and waiting until the last minute. My first year was a horror show of time-management failures that almost cost me my acceptance and status with the school. I really did not hit my stride until my junior year and only got back to solid *A*s and *B*s in my senior year. Because of setbacks (and having a job throughout school), it took me over five years to graduate.

Working under pressure is not a time-optimized strategy. Sure, there will be those situations where you will find the heaviness and burden of a deadline, even when you feel you have done a solid job of planning. However, the idea is to limit those instances because you decide to ingrain the attitude of preparation into everything you do.

In this book, we lead with *Planning*, not necessarily because it is the most important time-management category. We start here, because with time optimization, you need to start somewhere. The PEC of time optimization starts with *preparation*. Remember, a "continuous pursuit of the right preparation." The two go hand in hand, planning *and* preparation.

Planning is segmented into four subjects that are very broad but also very specific. *Personal Goals* run the gambit, from a life purpose statement down to short-term targets of less than a week. The mentality of *Mapping Ahead* safeguards your time and keeps you from falsely thinking you can "work best under pressure." Because *Meetings* play such an important role in our work life, there should be more planning, whether you are the facilitator or the participant. "Professionals average 21.5 hours in meetings a week, over half of the 'standard 40-hour work-week'."[1] Finally, *Completing Assignments*, or finishing what you start, may sound like an outcome and not an input. In time optimization, it is counted in planning because too many times, people do not get done what they start out to do.

A TIME-OPTIMIZED PLANNER—TRACY HOLMES

Tracy Holmes is a passionate person, which by extension makes him a passionate planner. I know this because I have worked with Tracy in two different companies for many years. In that time, I can't recall a single instance where he did not have a pen and some form of paper to write things down. Even on what were supposed to be personal occasions. If something came up, Tracy was ready to note it and go back and plan it. He embodies to me what can be found in Christian Scripture, in 2 Timothy 4:2: "Preach the word; be prepared in season and out of season; correct, rebuke and encourage—with great patience and careful instruction."[2]

In sales and sales management for over forty years, Tracy has managed just about any combination of teams. From small inside sales rep groups to hundreds of contract salespeople through multiple companies. Tracy does not buy into the traditional term of retirement, so today, he continues to lead a sales team, putting the same amount of energy and diligence into his work as he did when he took his first sales position.

I first realized Tracy's planning skills in his approach to meetings. Whether it was a simple one-on-one or an entire product launch training for the team, Tracy was not satisfied until he had clarity on every aspect of the topics to be discussed. As Tracy told me during the interview, "Time management is such a big deal to me because I do not like stress, and I can do something about it by planning and utilizing my days properly. I believe in doing both well." This allows him to be a man of his word and be seen as one who meets obligations.

Not only a strong planner in his professional life, Tracy and his wife Rhonda run a ministry focused on providing tools to help individuals and couples live extraordinary lives through the gifts God has given them.[3] To do that requires a lot of time and planning. "Time is an element given to us by God, and we need to take advantage of the time we have here on this earth to have a great impact to our families, career, and the passions that we have."

I wanted to feature Tracy in this chapter because, as he readily admits, he manages his time and plans *old-school*. You won't find elaborate project management software or sophisticated systems. What you will see is a man with a pen, a notepad, documents, and an electronic calendar, who passionately plans and re-plans. Don't get me wrong, he is not afraid to embrace contemporary tools, like a customer relationship management (CRM) system. He has demonstrated he can effectively use those for prospecting and client engagement. However, it is Tracy's focus on the basics that empowers him to bring clarity to the future, which then brings productivity in the present.

PERSONAL GOALS

I am not new to planning and setting goals. Spend any time in business and you will have a natural progression with first, getting to execute what is given to you; then you are invited to be involved in developing or providing input and ultimately moving to leading the establishment of goals.

As a new department store manager, I was given a sales goal and had my boss "looking over my shoulder," approving all merchandise buys. I met twice a month with the store manager, reviewing the details of my performance, and was given directions about changes I was to make.

Compare this to my last assignment (before I started my own company) where I was responsible for setting the sales strategy of four different companies. I did not do it alone; I sought advice from direct reports, and the board of directors would have final approval, but I had a lot of autonomy.

For so many years, what I lacked was true personal goals—ones I could call my own. It was not until my wife encouraged me to read a book called *Living Forward* by Michael Hyatt and Daniel Harkavy that it really hit home to me that I had no "personal" aspects connected with any goals.[4] They all seemed tied to business and career. This led us to both take a vacation day, set up in our dining room, and prepare our individual and private goals, based on the book and the supplemental materials accompanying *Living Forward*.

Since then, what I have realized—as I'm now tied to the time-optimized approach—is that everything you set is a personal goal. The distinguishing factor or question to clarify is this: "Is this a personal *personal* goal or is it a personal *career* goal?" In each instance, it is still personal.

Setting a time-optimized goal strategy starts large and wide. Then, through a series of evaluations and classifications, targets are identified and refined, depending on how long and detailed the planning needs to be. Encompassed within is the *P* in PEC. What preparation needs to be done to execute and maintain control? In addition, gaining clarity of the nature of the goal (linear or cyclical) must be refined to ensure getting over the finish line. Figure 3:1 illustrates the approach.

Goal Class	Length
Life Purpose Statement	Lifespan
Bucket List	3 Years to Lifespan
Long Term	1 to 3 years
Annual	Within a Calendar Year
Short Term	6 Months or Less

FIGURE 3:I GOAL CLASSES AND THEIR LENGTHS

You have probably figured out, depending on the nature of the goal, it will shift from one goal class to another as you get closer or further from the objective. In addition, the details and specifics become more defined as you near the culmination. In 2022, I had a bucket-list item (hiking the Grand Canyon from rim to rim) move to an annual goal and then back to settle in as a long-term one. Three changes in a thirty-day period. Time-optimized goal planning is fluid, active, and meant to be engaged and not static.

LIFE PURPOSE STATEMENT

I learned to save money at an early age, instilled in me by my parents. That has paid off (another intended pun) because we have a solid retirement portfolio. As our financial planners reviewed the details with us, I challenged myself and asked, "If I did not work, what would be my purpose in life?" It is not that I felt adrift—quite the contrary. I had a great job, marriage (still do), grounded children, a wonderful family, and fantastic friends. My principles are solid; I try to lead with good intentions, and I wish to function at high ethical standards. But that is not a refined declaration or testimony. I needed it to be well . . . time-optimized, something that can be prepared, ready to execute, and tied into my life and in which I have control over the outcome.

The process to craft your purpose statement is found in these steps. It requires an investment of focused time (talked about later in the book).

- What is my dream(s) for life? Is it or are they realistic?
- How would things be different if my life dreams come true?
- If I had no constraints on my resources, what would I like to do?
- If I have a spouse or significant other, does my dream connect on a personal level with them?
- What are my core values? What are my spouse's core values?
- What are my greatest personal strengths?
- What are three noteworthy things others would say about me?
- Where do I feel I will be in five years, ten years, twenty years?

Answering these questions allows you to build a short declaration. Here are a couple of templates:

My goal in life is to *[state your long-term vision]*, believing I can accomplish this by focusing on *[insert core values or most important core value]*.

I will have a fulfilled life because of *[insert core values]* based on my *[insert personal strengths]*.

I am so passionate about people having a life purpose and being able to share that with others. Therefore, at the end of the book in the Resources section, you will find a web address that will take you to a page to download a life purpose template so you can create your unique statement.

BUCKET LIST

The origin of the term "bucket list" is contemporary, based on the movie title of the same name. Released in 2007, the main characters, played by Jack Nicholson and Morgan Freeman, are both diagnosed with cancer and have a short time to live. They begin a journey to complete a list of activities before they "kick the bucket."[5]

Before you think this is some weird goal-setting process, the concept in time-optimized planning is a bit more structured and is not meant to be started when you have something wrong with you. It should be a fun exercise, where you can think about unconventional targets, unique aspirations, and any ambitions you have without any pressure of needing to carry them out in a specific timeline. This record of desired achievements is for old and young alike. It will be fluid and changing. In fact, a great place to start is with some of the dreams you wrote down in the development of your Life Purpose Statement.

Items for consideration are as limited as your imagination. The bucket list has no minimum or maximum number of goals. It can involve relationship ideas, like falling in love and getting married, or something more uncommon, like learning to parachute. The easiest place to begin is with travel—swim with dolphins or stay at the presidential suite of a fancy hotel. Don't discount career accomplishments. Running a Fortune 500 company is appropriate too.

What makes the time-optimized bucket list process a little different is how this interacts with your overall goal-setting strategy. You need to have at least some type of outline for each occasion because bucket-list options may move to become more defined goals. Therefore, enumerate them in this way.

- Rank by order of importance.
- Describe what you want to accomplish.
- Establish a start date.
- Jot down a quick summary of the resources you might need.
- Estimate a targeted completion date.

Do not get hung up if you don't know all the details; put down what you feel comfortable with. If it is important enough in the future, you will find that you will do more work to fill in the specifics.

I am jumping ahead right now, but I think it is important to mention how you maintain and adjust the bucket list after it has been made. Since most individuals will not be referring to this frequently, it is advantageous to create a system. Once again, I bring up PEC. Setting this list is the *preparation*. *Executing* the list at this point is knowing where to access it if you don't look at it for months. *Controlling* the list is how often you want to retrieve it to update it. This simple exercise involves task management and organization (calendar planning), both of which will be covered later in the book.

A well-developed time-optimized bucket list can make a significant impact on the subsequent goal-planning types. Intentionally hold yourself accountable to review and change your list to reflect the priorities of your life and anticipate what might come. If you treat this as a "one-off" exercise, you may find yourself planning other goals that reduce potential enriching opportunities. Instead of achieving these goals, you'll be kicking the can—I mean *bucket*—down the road.

LONG TERM

The goal-setting discussion to this point has been on the conceptual and even theoretical side. The Life Purpose Statement, while very important, may not provide concrete illuminations that fully deliver the answer to your existence. Similarly, as a pail typically holds liquid that moves around, a bucket list is meant to be fluid, naturally leading to changes and adjustments. In each instance (purpose and bucket), that is okay, and that is its intention. On the other hand, establishing extended ideas and missions is meant to be firmer and more purposeful. Time-optimized long-term goals are one or two years in length, with many milestones and sub-goals planned into the mix.

The most foundational personal productivity book for me is *Getting Things Done* by David Allen. I first read it years ago and have used and kept so many applications with me throughout my professional career. David introduces "The Natural Planning Model," where the mind goes through five steps to accomplish any task: defining the purpose and principles, outcome visioning, brainstorming, organizing, and identifying the next steps.[6] There is a sense of purpose and structure around the action.

While the *Getting Things Done* example is about tasks, I highlight it here to demonstrate the parallel nature of long-term goal setting. When you decide to establish one, you need to have a model to set yourself up for success. There is a level of seriousness and commitment you plan to apply. It is an understanding that "I will expend time in the future for an extended timeframe to achieve something important."

Long-term goals can be birthed out of your life purpose. They logically come from your bucket list. In fact, many times a long-term goal is a formalized bucket-list entry. They can exist in both places. As you begin to conceptualize your long-range plans, classify them into the right segment of your life, as shown in Figure 3:2.

Type	Explanation
Personal/Personal	Strictly tied to you and has no bearing on your career or profession
Personal/Professional	A special ambition or target outside your regular duties and responsibilities that will move you forward from your current career position
Professional	A goal tied to your business or employer that you choose to add to your individual goal-planning process

FIGURE 3:2 SEGMENTING TYPES OF GOALS

PEC gets applied here as well. The time-optimized long-term goal-planning approach is based on asking and answering these questions.

- What is the type of goal needed to be done? See Figure 3:1 (Preparation)
- Why do I want to do this? (Preparation)
- What is the length? (Preparation, Execution)
- How will I accomplish this? (Preparation, Execution)
- How do I measure progress? (Execution, Control)
- How will I track headway? (Execution, Control)
- What tools do I need? (Execution, Control)
- How will I evaluate? (Control)

In a compelling book on accountability called *The Oz Principle*, the authors write, "You can't create accountability without clearly defining results. You can't score a goal if you can't see the goal line. [A]t this stage, you want to talk in terms of results, not just activity."[7]

Addressing the questions and developing them into a formal plan ensure meeting the accountability standards referenced in *The Oz Principle*. Long-term goals should contain a layer of good tension that places ownership on you, regardless of the kind of goal (personal-personal, personal-professional, or professional).

The details around the goal should be seen in the tools you use in everyday time management (your planner, calendar, and journal).

I do not recommend setting a lot of long-term goals at once. They are meaningful, sophisticated, complex, and deep. While you may go for long periods without doing anything, when it comes time to work on a long-term goal, that time should be focused, intense, and productive. If you are unable to be rigid—and yes, accountable—evaluate the level of importance the goal is to you. Life is going to be filled with continuous annual and short-term goals and all the tasks that come along with them.

If you are new to this, start with one. "So many of us have set up too many goals only to find ourselves achieving few to none of them. It's just hard to handle everything at once."[8] Once you feel comfortable and understand the impact a lengthy aim has on your productivity, you can try to have one or two additional goals, but I do not recommend working more than three long-term goals at the same time.

ANNUAL

We all have events that we participate in every year. In my case, I have a goal to see my sons at least once each year. My wife (who will be giving you her time-management perspective in Chapter 9) has a goal of seeing our children at least three times each year. Guess which number wins?

Our kids each live half a country away in different parts of the United States. The preparation revolves around picking the dates, finding lodging, determining what is needed for the trip, deciding on the route (we usually drive), choosing who we want to see besides family, and solidifying the budget. When the time comes, we execute by packing the car well, driving safely to the destination, and completing what we want to accomplish (mainly spending time with the kids). Our control is to ensure we meet our desired outcomes in the time we are away from home and travel back safely.

Going back to Figure 3:1, an annual goal occurs within a particular calendar year or is a year in length. However, the preparation or establishment of the goal best happens at least three months before the start of that goal. Let me clarify.

Throughout my professional career, the month of September meant the engagement of annual planning for the next year. The revenue projection, along with all the necessary projects and expenditures needed, is intensely reviewed, adjusted, and finally formalized. An efficient and well-timed corporate plan gets approved around the beginning of November. However, there have been a couple of times the blueprint is not done until January or February of the next year, after the fiscal year has already begun.

Establishing annual goals for the next year in the time-optimized method encourages you to follow the business way and get your goals set at least sixty days before the end of a current calendar year for the next year. Why? Because there will be multiple types of goals, you need to plan that far ahead to pace out when and how they will all be completed. Check out Figure 3:3.

Preparation			Final Preparation, Execution, Control											
Oct	Nov	Dec	Jan	Feb	Mar	Apr	May	Jun	Jul	Aug	Sep	Oct	Nov	Dec

FIGURE 3:3 CALENDAR YEAR ANNUAL GOAL

Should you want to create an annual goal after the year is underway, use the same two-to-three-month gap from the creation to the start of that goal. See Figure 3:4 for an example.

Preparation			Final Preparation, Execution, Control											
Mar	Apr	May	Jun	Jul	Aug	Sep	Oct	Nov	Dec	Jan	Feb	Mar	Apr	May

FIGURE 3:4 ANNUAL GOAL OUTSIDE OF A TYPICAL CALENDAR YEAR

Annual goals can be around a single event six months into the year, or they can be for a series of events that occur over more than six months to achieve said goal. Yearly objectives are important occasions and of significant experience, which is why they take an investment of your time and use of PEC.

Like bucket-list items that can transition to long-term goals, so can long-term goals transition to annual goals. For example, you might choose to state, "My annual goal is to finish up the long-term goal I started last year." Similar to what we discussed in long-term planning, you will want to ask the following questions (weaving in PEC), to be answered some two-plus months before the goal is started.

- Why do I want to do this? (Preparation)
- What is the length? (Preparation, Execution)
- How will I accomplish this? (Preparation, Execution)
- How do I measure progress? (Execution, Control)
- How will I track headway? (Execution, Control)
- What tools do I need? (Execution, Control)
- How will I evaluate? (Control)

While annual goals are more rigid and formal, make sure they can bend and adjust. Set formal review and evaluation time. Anticipate what might happen if you complete one early or lag behind. Unlike the long-term goals that should be limited to one to two, depending on what you have planned, setting up to ten annual goals could be feasible. However, if you have not done a lot of annual goal-setting in the past, start small and work up.

SHORT TERM

I love spreadsheets. I think they are amazing instruments that allow us to do some powerful things. My passion came out of a short-term goal I created for myself after receiving promotion. I was moved into the position of district sales trainer, where I was responsible for teaching new sales representatives, along with coaching and instructing existing account managers. As technology began to play an increasing role in our jobs, there was a move away from paper to electronic reports. That meant Microsoft Excel was soon to be the tool of choice. I thought I should get a solid understanding of it if I was going to have any credibility with the team.

I set an immediate goal, simply stating, "I want to be the subject matter expert on spreadsheets in the district. I need to know more than anyone else." With the approval of my boss, I set aside one full day a week to have protected time where I did a deep dive on all things Excel. After six weeks (and I'll admit more hours on my own time), I had enough knowledge to answer questions as they came in from the field. That upfront investment has served me in too many ways to count throughout the rest of my career. It also sparked my passion for analyzing data and applying it to the sales process.

From Figure 3:1 again, short-term goals are for six months or less. I have found from personal experience and from leading teams, most of them are for three months or less. Like long-term and annual goals, there are a series of questions you need to ask and answer. Unlike the other two, short-term goals require a lot more specificity in all areas of PEC.

- What are the details? (Preparation)
- What are the hard start and stop dates? (Preparation, Execution, Control)
- What tools do I need? (Execution, Control)
- How much time will this take me? (Execution, Control)
- How will I allocate that time? (Preparation, Execution, Control)
- How will I track headway? (Execution, Control)
- What steps do I need to do to be fully committed? (Control)

The word *control* appears more in this process than in the others. Given the protracted amount of time, short-term goals scream for structure and time optimization. Your ability to control the events and the flow of that goal hinges on whether there has been serious consideration of the impact of your day-to-day routines along with the regular workload.

Finally, just to clarify: a short-term goal is not a task. Tasks are components of a goal. We will cover tasks and task management in the next chapter. Also, do not discount the importance of short-term goals. You may never know when a spreadsheet example like mine may turn into a career-marking moment.

GOALS ARE YOUR FRIENDS

On overall time-optimization thinking, goal setting is tightly linked to the *preparation* of PEC. Like an icebreaker ship that is designed to sail through ice-covered waters to create a clear passage, the establishment of benchmarks cuts through the noise of each day and opens pathways of time productivity.

Figure 3:5 helps show the interaction (or isolation) that occurs between types of goals.

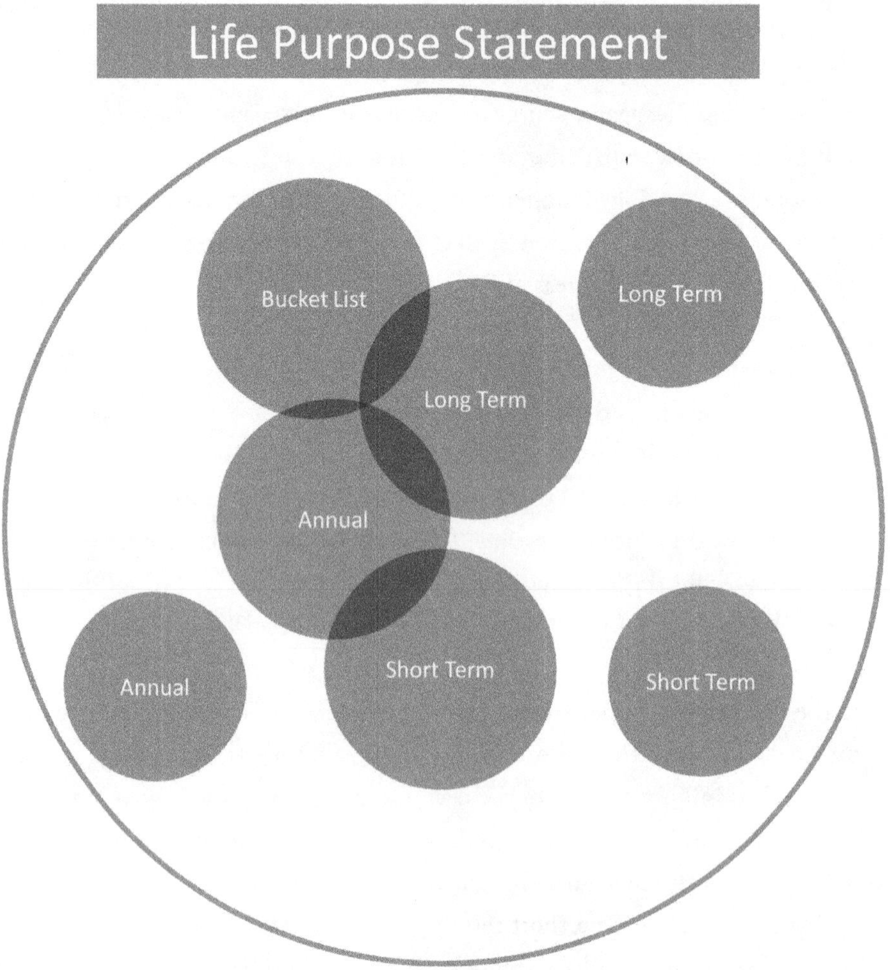

Life Purpose Statement

Bucket List

Long Term

Long Term

Annual

Annual

Short Term

Short Term

FIGURE 3:5 THE INTERACTION OF GOALS

All your goals should fit within the purpose you have created for your life. If any do not, immediately question the validity of that goal and decide if it needs to be adjusted or removed. As mentioned earlier in this section, bucket-list, long-term, and annual objectives can flow from one to the other or exist in more than one place. An annual goal can still be a bucket-list item. A variety of short-term goals might be tied to a single annual goal. Recognizing that many targets will not be generated from a bucket list, long- and short-term, as well as annual, goals can and will operate in isolation.

TRACY'S GOAL-SETTING WAY

Tracy is a daily goal-setting person. It is not an option for him. In fact, he blends the professional and personal probably better than anyone I know. Because he leads with his own goals, it is personal (play on words) to him.

Tracy confidently stated, "When it comes to setting my goals, God is first." That is a very direct purpose statement, and time is allocated to that first one—every single day.

Tracy's family was and still is weaved into short- and long-term goals. Tracy has two highly accomplished children. He and Rhonda have always aspired to help their children achieve greatness. That meant setting some lofty goals to get their kids in some of the best schools. Their hard work paid off. Today, goal setting is about meeting the immediate needs of his wife and children, but also about creating annual and long-term goals for his extended family and grandchildren.

That does not mean Tracy ignores the professional side of things. Though here, that might be seen as more automatic. I have seen Tracy participate in the planning process as we worked together (remember, he is always passionate); because of his servant-minded approach, business planning leans more toward ensuring he and his team can execute well.

One of the goal types I have not mentioned with Tracy is the *bucket list*. Tracy uses an approach called a *vision board*. I love this! "We want to be able to envision and imagine what your lives are going to be like. So we put up vision boards on mirrors or the wall—things we imagine or want to have. We look at this and meditate on these every single day," Tracy declared. Whether you use a bucket list or a vision board, follow Tracy and have it out in places where you see it frequently as a reminder and for inspiration.

MAPPING AHEAD

On the Time Management Analysis (TMA) assessment, one of the situations that must be answered is "I plan ahead." While only three words, and in essence, general in nature, time optimization cannot happen unless you really think forward and *prepare* (yup, back to PEC again). You might be thinking, "He talked a lot about preparation back in the goals section. Why is it needed here?" I wanted to keep *mapping ahead* separate from goals because goal setting (while encompassing your life) leans toward being a "head" exercise—particularly when you consider annual and short-term goals. Mapping ahead ensures you bring back the "heart" element because you are committing to yourself that you will plan, that you promise to make your goals, projects, and tasks a reality.

Do you think this is easier said than done? Consider the following statistics: "Less than 8% of people actually stick to their resolutions each year, according to some estimates, yet millions of Americans continue to set goals with high hopes of a better year ahead."[9] That is roughly 150 million people in the United States that started a resolution but did not finish.[10]

"In 2020, working-age baby boomers ages 56 to 64 were the most likely to own at least one type of retirement account (58.1%)."[11] More than 40 percent of those near the retirement age have done no structured retirement planning.[12]

Even when we try to have fun, it can be difficult. "Fewer than half of Americans (49%) take the time to plan their vacation days out each year, according to new research from Project: Time Off, held back by lack of certainty with personal schedules (64%), work schedules (57%), and children's schedules (50%)."[13] What a great example of the cascade effect of not charting forward in all areas of your life.

Mapping ahead is intertwined with many of the other elements of time optimization.

- As we already showed, it triggers details into your goal setting
- It provides a path to finish activities
- Your task management is much easier because you draw in the present to set the future
- Forget focus, upcoming events can become a murky pond filled with the odor of procrastination, distractions, and interruptions
- Working out front of due dates keeps organization tight
- When it comes to personal care (like exercise), if you don't plan ahead, it will probably not happen spontaneously

TRACY'S MAPPING AHEAD WAY

Coming back to my friend, if you remember what has been said about Tracy, his mind is always on the future. Planning forward is based on short-term, long-term, and vision projecting. Tracy tracks his progress in all three categories because he constantly invests time reviewing and discussing with his wife, family, and coworkers. He makes planning fully action-based and continuous, not event-centered.

Now, Tracy does clarify that much of his *mapping ahead* strategy is focused on one year out. It is easier for him to track, and as he said, "I like to be able to mark off the item; I love to be able to see the progress and those victories and milestones, and I can do that when I set a lot of my planning for one year."

MEETINGS

I have a huge appreciation for meetings. Generally, I really like them. Kind of bizarre, right? Well, if you are a person today who thinks, "Dave, I can really time optimize my time-management by doing away with about three-quarters of them," you are not alone. According to research done by *Harvard Business Review*, "92% of employees consider meetings costly and unproductive."[14]

Then why do I enjoy sitting in a room or participating through a computer screen with a bunch of other people? Because I know what constitutes a good meeting. I appreciate it when I am done with a well-run event, and I evaluate the poorly executed ones to see where I can improve when I lead my own. I have adopted the principles laid out in the book *Death by Meeting*.[13] If it wouldn't dishonor the author's work and violate who knows how many copyright laws, I would simply copy "The Model" section,[15] paste it right here, call it good, and go get an adult beverage. Instead, I simply share that if you struggle with meetings, whether individually or as a team, head to Patrick Lencioni's *Table Group* website and buy the book.[16]

If I am singing the praises of *Death by Meeting* so much, then what else do I have to say? Well, there are two areas of emphasis, whether you love or hate meetings. A time-optimized approach asks that you put effort into being *on time* and *prepared* for meetings because you have planned for meetings.

ON-TIME TO MEETINGS

In a 2018 survey done by the Tolina group, they observed 37 percent of the respondents noted the challenge late arrivals and early departures have on the flow and productivity of meetings.[17] Add in the data that "organizations spend roughly 15% of their time on meetings, with surveys showing that 71% of those meetings are considered unproductive."[18] This is a recipe for the degradation of productivity and morale.

You'll be reminded about this in Chapter 7 when we cover calendars in detail, but now is a good time to show you some time-optimized tips that align with, you guessed it, PEC.

- Preparation: Not all meetings are alike, depending on the importance of the appointment, so think about reserving buffer time before and after the event
- Preparation: Do not allow multiple meetings to be stacked one right after the other
- Preparation: Negotiate a new stretch if you are given a meeting time that you are not comfortable you can arrive promptly to
- Execution: Proactively communicate if you are running late or will be late
- Execution: If you have commitments back-to-back, inform the current members of your need to leave at a certain time to make another meeting
- Control: Should meetings be added to your schedule, invest the time and go back to the preparation stage to ensure you see about adjusting any prior commitments
- Control: Make your needs known. Your best intentions may not pan out. If you are concerned about your ability to be there, on the dot, then speak up

You may have noticed that all the examples noted above relate to participation. What about when you lead a meeting? The same PEC rules apply, only with even more heightened awareness. You'll not only have the burden of managing your schedule, but you must be mindful of the bearing your tardiness will have on the information you need to present to the others you have asked to come.

MEETING PRE-PLANNING

I started off the *Planning* section back in Chapter 2 with, "Pre-planning prevents poor performance." I can't think of a better example to apply that little proverb to than your participation and leadership in meetings. Yes, you heard right; you should never consider a meeting an opportunity to be only a spectator. Always look for an opportunity to be a contributor. I realize not all meetings afford the chance to furnish your thoughts. However, the question should always be asked, "What do I need to get out of this meeting?" That is the definitive *control* question.

To time optimize the set-up process for meetings, get in the habit of reasoning through the items in Figure 3:6.

Pre-planning Steps	Leader	Participant
Do I really need to have this meeting?	✓	
Set a clear objective (What do I need to get out of this meeting?)	✓	
Create a meeting agenda	✓	
Determine length	✓	
Decide on people	✓	
Establish the time	✓	
Send request, including objective, agenda, length, people, and time	✓	
Review objective and agenda		✓
Do I really need to attend this meeting?		✓
What do I need to get out of this meeting?		✓
Ask any pre-meeting questions of the facilitator		✓
Answer pre-meeting questions	✓	
Come ready to contribute	✓	✓
Come ready to ask questions and allow additional perspectives	✓	✓

FIGURE 3:6 THE MEETING PLANNING RESPONSIBILITIES OF THE LEADER AND PARTICIPANT

I could carry the list on and add how you should conduct and/or participate in the meeting—in addition to end-of-meeting assignments and post-follow-up. Yet, this is only about what time optimization looks like for everyone *before* the event. The entire meeting cycle will intertwine with the task management and organization chapters.

TRACY'S MEETING WAY

Having spent many hours in the same meetings with Tracy, I never saw him unprepared, whether as the leader or a participant. Indeed, I knew that if Tracy was in a meeting I led, I better be ready, or I was going to be asked a question I might not know the answer to. It was not because Tracy sought "*got you*" moments; he was committed to knowing what role he might be in the follow-up after a meeting.

Agendas are the key starting or jumping-off points for any meeting for Tracy. If you don't have an agenda, he'll ask for one. If he leads, he sends one out in advance.

It does not matter if Tracy is the organizer or member, his mission is "to understand the needs of the person as well as the activity. I believe they go hand in hand. The business is important, but I need to understand the person in front of me, their heart, their thinking—to make sure that aligns with what they need to accomplish or what I need to accomplish. If I can get those two things to happen, I believe we will have a very productive meeting."

COMPLETING ASSIGNMENTS

I was in a retail store-management training program and was moving through it well. Then I was asked to complete what is called an "assortment plan." It is a detailed project where you develop the product mix and determine the sales impact for the next selling season. I was not given a hard deadline, but I was not going to move forward in the system until I turned it in to the instructor.

Because there were a lot of steps involved, I kept delaying the undertaking (procrastinating really—a lot more on that later). There was always something more fun to do. At one point, the trainer challenged me to turn in my assignment. I became motivated, buckled in, reserved the time, and powered through the project. I received accolades and praise for my work and the thoroughness of my analysis. However, because I dawdled, I cost myself a spot in the promotion rotation and had to stay in the training program for an additional two weeks.

In Chapter 6, we will talk about *internal focus*, the areas of time optimization that point the finger back at you or encourage you to pick up a mirror and look at yourself to see what needs to change. Completing assignments is another internal impetus to overcome. I have led employees who always seemed to be tardy and work with clients that almost make it a habit to be late with their work. In the book, *The Power of Habit*, Charles Duhigg explains, "[T]o modify a habit, you must decide to change it. You must consciously accept the hard work of identifying the cues and rewards that [drive] the habits' routines, and find alternatives."[19]

Usually, a breakdown in the ability to complete work, tasks, or projects is not an isolated incident. It may not be categorized as a negative habit, but there are certain time-management challenges that preclude the motivation to get your stuff done on time. If that is the case for you, I bring you back to *preparation* in PEC in Figure 3:7.

	Prioritize activity against current demands and obligations
	Understand the scope of the job
	Reduce into smaller, more manageable segments
Assignment Preparation	Create tasks with identified start and stop dates
	Translate tasks into blocks of protected time on your calendar
	Negotiate any protected time
	Know the milestones to be reached that will keep you on schedule
	Get an accountability partner to hold you accountable

FIGURE 3:7 THE STEPS TO PREPARE TO COMPLETE AN ASSIGNMENT

I learned my assortment plan lesson. It did not fully cure me of the tardy bug, but I realized execution before preparation meant I could not control my time as well.

TRACY'S ASSIGNMENT WAY

You have probably figured out this fact by now, but I am going to tell you that Tracy gets done what he needs to do on time. "I am very task-oriented. If I have planned it and set it as an A-level priority, I have already done the research and put in the appropriate amount of energy beforehand, to where it is going to be finished on time."

Tracy pressures himself to complete major goals early. If he has seven days, he'll try to complete it in five. This affords him the opportunity to review it (one more time) before he considers it done. Tracy also wants to honor his word and commitment to himself and to others who will be relying on him.

Knowing there might be an occasion when he will be unable to finish, Tracy does not wish or guess. If he owes something to someone else, he immediately discusses the status of his activity and seeks clarity from the assigner about possible date changes. I've never known Tracy to just ignore a due date or hope that it would be forgotten.

BE A TOP—TIME-OPTIMIZED PLANNER

Chapter 3 has covered a lot of ground. We will go into detail in Chapter 10 when we discuss the time-optimized life and just where TOP (time-optimized planning—look, another acronym!) plays into that. To foreshadow, planning and the preparation of PEC are connected. Personal goals are all about aligning your future with your desires, wishes, and aspirations. Mapping ahead is also about the upcoming but in a deliberate and known way. The outcome might be uncertain but not the mode. Meetings in a TOP approach are about the immediate, imminent, and impending. If you don't prepare, forget about execution and control. Finally, missed assignments can be an injurious habit. Reduce the chances of harm; challenge your internal self to ease the external tests of execution and control.

While much of the effort you put into time-optimized planning has a look and feel of a linear time-thinking worldview, remember that poor planning on the front end may actually cycle you back to the beginning to revamp and readjust. With the right attitude, you will receive a great education, minimizing making the same mistakes again. Yet, take planning seriously now, and the cycle will be a continuous improvement moving forward, without having to go back to go forward.

CHAPTER 4

Time-Optimized Task Design

*The ability to multitask might seem important, but I think
that people don't recognize (me included), you can't really
effectively multitask and get anything done efficiently.*
(Matt Anselmo)

Back in Chapter 2, I let you peek into my marriage to see how differently Susan and I approach organization. I am neater and more structured. However, when it comes to finding what you need, she'll get there quicker than me. Well, I am back at it again. As managing tasks go, we could not be any more different.

I am fully electronic, setting tasks on the computer and syncing them with my phone and tablet. Susan is all about paper. Whether it is on a calendar, in a planner, or on a list, she has it written down.

Some of the biggest arguments in our marriage (we are blessed because we really don't quarrel) happened with the process of cleaning up. I would throw away a list that she was working from to complete activities.

Early in the relationship, when said challenges arose (on a problem I created in the first place), I would feel the need to "coach" her on the benefits of electronic task management. I encouraged Susan, telling her digital lists will never be lost because they are safely stored . . . not on paper. In fact, she could even share and assign me tasks to get done and track my progress! Somehow, my assistance and help were never quite appreciated in those moments. I am a fast learner and know in the heat of marital differences, it is better to listen and learn rather than teach and train.

Today, we are basically in the same place in our marriage with task management. I am all in with electronic, and she is all on paper. The good news is that both of us still manage to get our tasks completed. So, while I encourage everyone to embrace a digital task mindset, I realize people can be organized and productive by writing everything down.

A TIME-OPTIMIZED TASK ADMINISTRATOR—MATT ANSELMO

I have known Matt since high school, and at this point, we have been close friends (really, like brothers) for decades. He is a Proverbs 17:17 kind of guy: "A friend loves at all times, and a brother is born for a time of adversity."[1] I could fill pages of stories that have no bearing on time optimization that would humor the author and the subject but probably make the rest of you close the book and move on (maybe even in disgust). So, to keep you engaged, let me tell you about his abilities to accomplish his tasks well.

Matt's vocation helped set the table for how he has established his current task abilities. Like many of us, he began his career in retail and worked his way into a management role with a major drugstore chain. Matt realized, "I did not want to live to work." As a result, he sought a better work-life balance. At that time, the term would simply have been "free time." That led him into a long, successful career in sales in a variety of different roles and industries.

Sales can be a task-driven occupation, particularly when you first start out. Matt assumed leadership positions that forced him to not only manage his tasks, but to ensure subordinates were managing theirs.

When I interviewed Matt and we got into the details about task administration, he immediately talked about what items are important and knowing them as you head into the day—and then looking ahead as the current day ends. He naturally blends those priorities between his personal and professional life. Matt has had to make this a necessity because he has had plenty of practice. With a blended family and being an involved parent of two sets of twins (that is not a typo, four girls), additional stepdaughters, and a stepson, my friend needed to figure something out just to stay sane and be an engaged father.

Because of this, task structure and isolation are critical. His formula is to "understand what your priorities are, organize your day around those priorities, and then focus [on getting done] what you can." Notice how he implies that not everything may get completed. Part of his planning process is to "recognize, sometimes it is okay if you do not get something done. It goes back to work-life balance, [and] that is very important to me." He can afford to feel that way because he (unknowingly to this point) uses a PEC method. Matt's *preparation* is prioritization; his *execution* is his focus. His *control* is looking at his records twice a day and having a mindset that the world will not end because everything does not get checked off.

We'll return to Matt throughout the chapter as he provides us with his perspective, which may not align directly with my viewpoints but are practical, real-life applications.

MAINTAINING A TASK LIST

I quoted Benjamin Franklin earlier in the book, using a couple of references to help frame the definition of time management. Because managing his time was so important, it is not surprising that he would have a solid system in place. Franklin was so committed that he is a "great example of someone known for using lists to encourage his own self-improvement. He famously detailed a thirteen-week plan to practice important virtues such as cleanliness, temperance, etc. Each day he tracked his progress on a chart."[2] In addition, it was also noted that he suffered from setting too many goals, and, at times, they were in conflict with each other.[3] I don't know about you, but I feel a bit comforted knowing someone like Benjamin Franklin struggled with too many things on the list and wondering which ones took priority.

I think I have done just about every type of to-do or task list you can think of in existence (I know, overstating it). Daily sheets of paper, spiral notebooks, composition books, journals, legal pads, graph paper (yup, that's right), note pads, memo pads, notecards, Post-it notes, wall calendars, personal calendars, monthly planners, daily planners, Franklin Planner[4] (inspired by you know who), Microsoft Outlook Tasks[5], Google Tasks[6], *Full Focus Planner*[7], and a whole host of other online and manual tools.

Based on the vast number of options and permutations of resources, it may seem like an impossible task (another pun intended) to land on one particular way. I have an easy means to start to narrow the choices since we are just getting into the chapter. It is again time to bring up PEC (yay!). Think about your current task list structure and ask yourself these three questions:

1. Am I able to *prepare* a task list that is realistic, reflects the needs I must complete, and is set in such a way I can make easy changes and updates?
2. Do I consistently *execute* my task list in such a way that I complete all my tasks in the time I allocated and by the dates I established?
3. Does my task list have a way for me to *control* my time, or do I find myself reacting and readjusting my list because it was not planned out as well as I liked?

If you happened to answer positively to all three, don't jump ahead yet. There will be plenty for you to consider along the way to Chapter 5. However, I will mention to you as we move forward, I have a preferred way to achieve time optimization, but if you can meet your PEC needs with your current task system (even if it is Post-it notes), I salute you. Just do not be afraid to explore other options because learning is never wasted time.

Now, if you were unable to answer yes to the PEC of task-list maintenance, let's walk through a system to consider. It will be electronic and not paper in nature. I am placing attention on this format because I feel it saves hours over the course of a year. Paper planners are functional and totally acceptable time-optimized instruments. However, handwriting the updates does take more time. Flipping back and forth consumes more effort. Electronic planning makes things like date changes, adding notes, splitting tasks, combining tasks, forwarding to-dos, categorization, and grouping more efficient.

Apple, Gmail, and Outlook account for over 90 percent of the email clients used worldwide. Expand to the top ten and it reaches almost 97 percent.[8] That just about guarantees whatever email system you are using today has a calendar and task system already built into the service. Right now, you have two foundational and extremely effective time-management tools. Given the robust nature of the app market, these same tools are available for phone and tablet, so you can sync activities across multiple devices. For our discussion here, I am going to limit the conversation to the big three, since their capabilities parallel and even overlap each other.

Because software is ever-changing and updating, I will stay at a high level with this discussion. If you are reading this a few years after the publishing date, I want you to be able to create your task list and have it work well. In addition, each program still has its differences, as they try to offer unique characteristics.

Another item for deliberation: I prefer to do any planning or heavy task maintenance on as large a screen as possible. You get a better view and can manipulate the data easier and faster. Your phone is good for completing single or more focused items, like closing out a task or adding one. If one of my children were looking over my shoulder right now, they might tell me, "That is because you are a boomer." Ultimately, I get it; you'll land on what works best for you.

At any rate, we will journey our way through task maintenance by (shock of all shocks!) using PEC (insert sarcastic emoji).

TASK PREPARATION AND GROUNDWORK

Digital tasking works best when a foundation has been set. That starts with categories or what many of the programs simply like to call "lists." You may be confused about the word *list*. A full record of all your tasks is one long list. When we speak of *lists,* think "groups" or "classifications." They allow you to place individual tasks into a cluster of similar to-dos, permitting better tracking, ranking, and arranging. Today, your overall task list might be imagined like Figure 4:1. You have them out there, know they have to get done, but are unsure where to start.

```
○ Task 5    ○ Task 1    ○ Task 2
○ Task 12   ○ Task 7    ○ Task 15
○ Task 8    ○ Task 14   ○ Task 4
○ Task 3    ○ Task 6    ○ Task 13
○ Task 10   ○ Task 9
```

FIGURE 4:1 UNCATEGORIZED TASKS

Should grouping your overall tasks into smaller lists (again, think categories) be new to you, then less is more. Limit your categories to general groups. Decide what are important areas of your life (personal and professional) and start there. Typically, a good place to begin is with:

- **General Personal Activity:** That's right, a true time-optimized task list contains all elements of your life. Integrating whole facets will make prioritizing much easier when we get to that discussion.
- **General Professional Activity:** Include the day-to-day elements you need to do what is expected of you and help you excel in your work.
- **Short-Term and Annual Goals:** Drawing on the goal information in Chapter 3, place elements of your time-appropriate goals here. There can be multiple tasks tied to one goal.
- **Miscellaneous:** Whatever you do not feel can be placed in a specific area, set in here.

For those time-optimized star pupils, you might be thinking, "Why didn't he mention the life purpose, bucket list, and long-term goals as well?" I am so proud of you. They were intentionally left off because a task list is about movement and implementation. If you have not touched a bucket list item for five years, let it stay there. Just remember to set yourself a task under General Personal Activity that says "Update Bucket List" at least once a year. Now, taking the uncategorized task illustration and placing them in the common sets, your tasks could look like Figure 4:2.

General Personal Activities	General Professional Activity	Annual Goals	Short-Term Goals	Miscellaneous Activity
○ Task 7	○ Task 1	○ Task 4	○ Task 12	○ Task 8
○ Task 3	○ Task 9	○ Task 15	○ Task 14	○ Task 10
○ Task 6	○ Task 5			
○ Task 2	○ Task 13			
	○ Task 11			

FIGURE 4:2 TASKS LISTS OR CATEGORIES

I know nothing gets past the readers of this book. You are correct; the tasks are not arranged in order. Figure 4:2 hints a little toward prioritization, which we will cover in the next section. Suffice it to say, not all tasks are equal, and laying out which tasks are important is a key element of preparation.

I need to introduce dates into the equation. I could have done it earlier, but I felt the need to emphasize the importance of categories or listings because that may have a bearing and flexibility on your due dates. Electronic tasks typically have three date properties: the reminder date, the due date, and the recurring date.

Date Type	Description
Reminder	Use this to activate a reminder of when to begin or continue a task. A lot of times, people will schedule the reminder on the same day the task is due. If that is intentional, no issues. However, should you need more time than one day to complete, schedule it earlier to remind yourself of the right time to start
Due	Whether expectations have been set by you or from someone else, the due date is your commitment to complete the task
Recurring	Sometimes the same kind of task is repeated over and over again. Creating a replica that is automatically generated once the due date is reached (even if the current task is not done), saves time and reduces the chances of missed assignments

FIGURE 4:3 TASK DATE TYPES

Expanding our example from Figure 4:2, here is what happens to the categories when we account for the dates and any repetitions. There is a clear sense of what must be completed first.

A common time-management snag is people treating their tasks like an "all you can eat buffet" restaurant they dine in every day. Let's say you are visiting your favorite place called the Task Bistro Buffet. You walk up to the counter and fill your dish with all this great-looking food (don't forget the desserts). With a full plate, you head back to your table and begin to enjoy it—only to find halfway into the meal you are full. There is still a lot of food left. Thankfully, the eatery offers you a to-go box, and you load up the remaining meal and think, "I'll just save it for tomorrow." At home, you open your refrigerator and place the carton in there with all the other left-over meals from previous days. Some of the food in those containers might even get spoiled. The next day, you wake up refreshed, pass by the refrigerator on your way out the door, and head back to the buffet for a new meal, and the cycle starts all over again. Remembering our worldview discussion in Chapter 1, this is a bad example of the cyclical function of time.

A rudimentary approach to creating and managing tasks relies on knowing your hunger level before you sit down to eat. If you consistently finish your tasks and are a member of the "clean plate club," then press ahead, since you know your appetite for the number of tasks you can handle. However, when there are still items left at the end of the day, you are planning too much and need to start out with a smaller plate. We will integrate tasks with all other aspects of time-optimization later in the book. For right now, set a lower number of tasks each day (start out with an appetizer) and add more tasks (go back to the buffet) as you finish up the previous ones.

Continuing with our eating analogy . . . "Desmond Tutu once wisely said that 'there is only one way to eat an elephant: a bite at a time.' What he meant by this is that everything in life that seems daunting, overwhelming, and even impossible can be accomplished gradually by taking on just a little at a time."[9] The same can be true of a task. Too many times, people try to take a mini project or multi-step task and make it an elephant of an activity.

With the advantage of a digital task method, you can take a sophisticated assignment and break it down into a series of sub-tasks or steps (see Figure 4:5). These should only be applied to activities beyond what is due on the current date. Setting multiple steps for one task on the day the item is due puts you right back at the buffet. If the elephant still seems too big because there are so many steps to the task, then it sounds more like a short-term goal, which probably contains a series of independent undertakings.

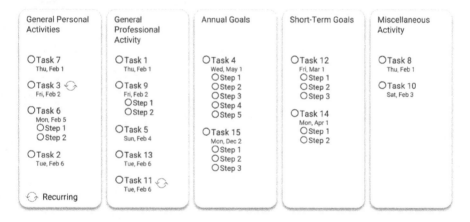

FIGURE 4:5 TASKS LISTS OR CATEGORIES WITH ADDED DATES, RECURRENCES, AND SUB-TASKS

I hope I have not made you hungry or sick to your stomach with task preparation and deciding the right groundwork to implement appropriately. As you create tasks, you'll want to set them into the right category or list, arrange them in the order of importance, determine the completion date, establish a reminder to start, and include any steps or sub-tasks.

Take a breath. We are done with the *P* of PEC on maintaining a task list; now let's tackle the *E* and see how we unceasingly execute an ever-changing task inventory.

TASK EXECUTION AND EFFORT

If "tasking" was a static endeavor, I would have a sentence here that said, "Thanks for stopping by . . . move along." Lucky for you (or not), maintaining a task list is a dynamic exercise—one that requires continuous (in the time-optimized definition) engagement and monitoring. Items flow in, stay for a period of time, maybe get adjusted, are completed and gone, or are completed and reincarnated as a repetitive obligation. Your tasks need a little TLC from you: tender, loving, care. From the time they are on your radar, be mindful they do not change or get lost.

When we last left our tasks laid out in Figure 4:5, they were neatly tucked away in their lists or categories, aligned by their due dates, noted with steps or subtasks, and fit for any recurrences. While they are organized that way for preparation, the tasks are best worked by viewing them by day, like on Figure 4:6.

FIGURE 4:6 TASKS ARRANGED BY DATE

To reemphasize, task preparation gets done in the category mode, while task execution gets done in the date mode. Don't worry, your digital calendar system will allow you to easily switch back and forth on a desktop monitor, laptop, or tablet display. Tasks can be closed out without difficulty and simple ones created from your mobile device. Working your to-dos is also focused on the more immediate tasks. The ones that typically fall outside a week or more stay in the planning phase. Based on that, let's pretend our most pressing tasks fall between 2/1 and 2/6 from Figure 4:7.

FIGURE 4:7 THE IMMEDIATE TASKS

As you survey the week, confirm again that you feel comfortable with the amount and type of each task that needs to be done. Tasks 6 and 9 each have two steps or sub-tasks. Confirm with yourself if you can get both phases completed in one day. Assuming you can't, your week might be adjusted to look like Figure 4:8.

FIGURE 4:8 THE IMMEDIATE TASKS, ADJUSTING FOR MULTISTEP TASKS

Once you have settled the week, you ought to begin each morning (or the start of your shift) reviewing the list of tasks and looking for the times when you will dedicate yourself to completing them. The process should be repeated at the end of the workday to check execution and make any adjustments. The way a week begins is not the way the week ends. That is fine if you stayed committed to completing your tasks.

TASK HANDLING AND CONTROL

Rounding out the PEC of maintaining a list is handling and control. I alluded to "task command" just a second ago. Look back at what you have just read in this section. There are a lot more words devoted to preparation and groundwork. That is a necessary step to be able to perform. Execution and effort were much shorter, not because they are less important but because the preparation allows for easy execution. That can only happen if you discipline (control) yourself. Remember, time-optimization is not switching from one aspect of PEC to another but using them together as *one* through the entire process.

Task Preparation

Time-
Optimized
Time
Task
Management

Task Execution   Task Control

FIGURE 4:9 TIME-OPTIMIZED TASK MAINTENANCE

MATT'S PERSPECTIVE

Let's return to my buddy, Matt. I have just gone through a detailed process to create, maintain, and optimize your duties or obligations electronically. Matt's primary task-organizing tool is his calendar. If it is a priority, it gets logged and set there. The rest he tracks off-line from a managed list.

"To me—maybe because it is that I am getting older—there are so many priorities, so many tasks, and things to track . . . [That] is life. [But] if I don't have it have it down somewhere, whether in my phone or on my computer (because [if] it is on the calendar, it pops up), I am going to miss something." Matt summarizes.

We will talk in depth later in the book on calendar management, but I do like Matt's example because it highlights the impact and positive role your calendar can play in task optimization.

PRIORITIZING TASKS

New York Times best-selling author Dave Ramsey, a trusted voice on money and business, says of working tasks, "A very simple but time-honored method to manage your day before it begins is the prioritized to-do list. Each morning, make a list of your activities that need to be done today. Then look at that list and ask yourself which items must be done *today*."[10] That seems pretty easy, right? Not for 59 percent of the people who took the Time Management Analysis assessment. In actuality, 13 percent don't even bother to prioritize.

To mess with your appetite again, I want to bring back the buffet analogy. I can understand you now saying, "Gosh, I get it—don't fill up the plate and don't take the leftovers home. Enough of the food comparison, please." Yes, I hear you and appreciate that, but let me continue anyway.

You're back at the Task Bistro Buffet and in front of all the food choices. The PEC of task optimization is on your mind (or food optimization, if you want to make it 'literal). You have a good idea of how much you can eat. There is an awareness not to take any leftovers home. You choose an appetizer, salad, two side dishes, a main course, and a dessert. Satisfied, you head to the table, get yourself seated, and wonder where to start.

Knowing you have a "sweet tooth," you begin with dessert. Enjoying that, next up is the appetizer. You recognize someone across the room and decide to visit with them for a bit. Coming back, you are still happy with your progress. Surveying what is left, you next munch on one of the side dishes, followed by the salad. Then a friend stops by the table, and you talk for a while. It is good to fellowship while you let the food settle. You conclude your conversation only to be told by the maître d' that the diner will be closing in five minutes. Still in front of you remains the main part of the meal and the lingering side dish. Pressed for time, you wolf down the side order, and then you guessed it: you ask for a to-go box for the main course.

When we began our fictitious meal, you had six dishes (tasks) to eat (complete). You managed to get five of them done, or over 80 percent. That makes it easy to say that the dinner (day) was productive. Except, you still need to figure out what to do with the main part of the meal (most important task). Truly prioritizing would have meant guaranteeing the most crucial aspect was eaten (accomplished). At the end of the meal, figuring out what to do with the dessert (lower-level task) is simpler.

When eating a meal, I am not suggesting you skip the appetizer and start with the main course, but when you decide to complete a task, begin with the most important one first.

All right, enough of the diet comparison. Let's get more practical. Too many times, people establish a list of tasks and start with the easiest ones first. Simple tasks give a false sense of accomplishment because, again, not all tasks are equal. There was a reason why I did not place the tasks in order on the examples we went through in the last section. Tasks should not be set by alphabetical order but by priority (preparation). We all have the best intentions at the start of our day, but interruptions and changes are bound to happen. It is better to have the easy tasks at the bottom and the significant to-dos set at the top.

Getting the harder or prominent tasks done first keeps you in a better frame of mind when they are all not finished on a given day. "[I]t's a good idea to adjust your explanations when you (inevitably) miss deadlines." Another best-selling author on leadership and change, Carey Nieuwhof, writes, "I used to say things like 'I didn't have a chance to get to it.' These days I say things like 'I'm really sorry. I didn't make the time to complete the project. That's my bad. Let's talk about how I can turn that around.'"[11] Notice the PEC aspect around this quote. After missing a time limit, the attitude (after the apology) goes right back to *preparation* to set up a new *execution*, scheduling with a commitment to better *control*. Nieuwhof is speaking externally here, but that is an appropriate conversation to have with yourself.

In my paper task-planning days, the traditional way to prioritize tasks was by the Franklin Planner process.

> *The Franklin Planner prioritizing process is simple. Take a look at your task list, sort out all the tasks with lettered priority labels: A for your top priorities, B for your next priorities, and so on. After assigning a letter to each task, prioritize each task in each letter group with a number. Start by selecting the next most urgent of the A priorities and assign that task with a 1, leaving A! next to your task. Continue [to] number all of the A tasks, and then start again with 1 in the B group.*[12]

When this gets executed well, it is time-optimized gold. My challenge was always investing enough time in the planning that I ended up with poor execution and then a loss of control.

While there are software options that parallel the Franklin Planner, the digital way of task optimization uses the standard email exchange offerings mentioned at the beginning of the chapter. They are simpler in design and do not use the lettering and number system. Risking dating myself, at the time of this writing, Apple-based *Reminders* allows for low, medium, or high designations. Microsoft *To Do* for desktop or your *Google Calendar* (adding the task bar off to the right) allows you to set by highlighting a star to make it important. In all cases, you can rearrange the order to show the most important at the top.

FIGURE 4:10 STARRING THE MOST IMPORTANT TASKS TO COMPLETE.
BLACK STARS REPRESENT PRIORITY TASKS

As you implement prioritization, remember that the beginning of the week will not look like the end of the week after you make the adjustments. Changes will come. What hopefully will happen is that all the tasks you set out to complete are done, though maybe not in the order you started. If you were really productive, there might even be more room to add some additional foods (tasks), or if your eyes were bigger than your stomach (available productivity), it is just a dessert and appetizer that are leftover.

MATT'S TAKE

Going back to our earlier conversations with Matt, I'll remind you that he repeatedly mentioned prioritization. It is foundational to his success in meeting commitments.

At one point during our interview, I was moving onto the next question, when Matt stopped me to provide a great tip. In a professional setting, we are faced with our priorities, but we are also impacted by the important concerns or needs of others. Therefore, he established a rule for him to always know the top five priorities of his boss, and as a leader, he constantly communicated to his direct reports his top priorities.

Matt also looks at his tasks, particularly the ones that make it on his calendar process, as a personal commitment he has made, not only to possibly someone else but to himself. Therefore, it is important to his honor and integrity that he finishes.

MULTITASKING (NOT)

Back in Chapter 2, when I first introduced multitasking, I left a teaser out there about a musician that can play an instrument and sing at the same time. It takes a ton of hours of practice in both areas. However, I don't consider listening to the radio while I drive multitasking. I can sing (again not well) to a song while I mosey on down the road, but I do not consider that being productive. It is annoying to anyone who hears me, although my primary focus and attention is on operating the vehicle. I have been able (through thousands of hours behind the wheel) to switch my attention quickly back and forth—singing to piloting.

So let's just go ahead and define multitasking, starting with a couple of straight dictionary definitions to keep it simple.

> *"the performance of multiple tasks at one time"*[13]
> *"a person's or product's ability to do more than one thing at a time"*[14]

Pretty straight forward, right? What's the big deal?

Let me add a *time-optimized* take on it.

> **Multitasking is the ability to think you can do more than one thing at a time, giving 100 percent of your attention to each task at the same time.**

When it comes to being productive, the desire to multitask is detrimental, not beneficial.

I can't help myself; I am taking you back to our favorite restaurant, the Task Bistro Buffet. Once again, you have gotten your items and brought them to the table. Excellent! You've learned from the last section and have laid out the dishes in the order in which you plan to consume the food.

Then you think, "Wait, I can be more efficient and eat two at the identical moment and lower the chance that I will have leftovers." You initially decide on the main course and the dessert. Quickly rethinking your strategy, you choose to switch to the salad and dessert because it is easier to eat the smaller ones.

Remember, we are all about PEC here. As you prepare to eat, how will you dine on both simultaneously? Will it be one fork loaded with both items or two separate forks with each food put in your mouth at the same time? How's that going to taste, by the way? I hope it doesn't cause a tummy ache. Should that happen, you'll be back to taking leftovers home. You executed badly (maybe got ill in the process) and lost control (I really thought about some type of bathroom analogy here but stopped myself).

I have had too much fun with this; let's bring in others that are a lot smarter than me and tackle this with a more serious tone.

THE CASE AGAINST MULTITASKING

Psychology Today gets direct. "Humans do not multitask well, and when a person says that he or she does multitask well, he or she is probably wrong. The human brain can only focus on one thing and one thing only at a time."[15]

"In multitasking, a computer never performs more than one task at a time, but the processing ability of the computer's processors is so fast and smooth that it gives the impression of performing multiple tasks at the same time."[16]

"[W]hen our brain is constantly switching gears to bounce back and forth between tasks—especially when those tasks are complex and require our active attention—we become less efficient and more likely to make a mistake," states health provider Cleveland Clinic.[17]

As written in the *Harvard Business Review*, "Interestingly, because multitasking is so stressful, single-tasking to meet a tight deadline will actually reduce your stress. In other words, giving yourself less time to do things could make you more productive and relaxed."[18]

Finally, best-selling author and keynote speaker Carey Lohrenz, writing in *Forbes* states, "If you're not focusing on the one thing that matters most right now—in other words, if you're not actively determining and then prioritizing what is most important—you're working against your own precious cognitive energies and diluting your power."[19]

I could go on and on. You could also do an internet search yourself on "the case for multitasking" and find counterpoints as well. To echo my perspective, *time-optimized time management* looks at multitasking as a negative attribute and a behavior to be avoided. The more you recognize you are switching between tasks, the more you can develop behaviors to take advantage of that. So don't close the book in disgust (hopefully, that didn't happen back with the Task Bistro Buffet example). Hear me out in the next section.

THE CASE FOR MICRO-TASKING

I was giving a time-management workshop for the pastoral staff of the church where I am a member. The senior minister (who you will meet later in the book), the Rev. Dr. Hunter Camp, challenged me, "Dave, can we talk about multitasking a second? I really think I do it well. I am able to have multiple tasks open and work them at the same time."

I responded with a question, "Hunter, are you really doing them at the same time, or are you really good at switching your focus between the tasks?" When we discussed the *time-optimized multitask* perspective, that made sense to him. Now, my pastor is a highly productive person, and has a strong ability to focus. Through the nature of his job and the many people he must serve, he has developed a knack of being highly concentrated in brief durations. He can micro-task.

The *time-optimized time management* definition states the following: *Micro-tasking is the ability to switch between tasks quickly, giving one task 100 percent of your attention and making progress before moving back to the previous task or adding another one.*

If you are thinking that sounds like how you operate, then fine-tune and hone in on spotlighting a single task. Give it your all for that short period and be mindful of shifting full attention to the next or even previous task. As you do this, pay attention to how much time it takes you to become fully committed.

To the rest of us (I fully admit, I can't switch easily), just plan out and execute our task-optimized strategy, one at a time. At the end of the day, if your to-do list is done, be satisfied and happy. There are no style points for getting there because you thought you could multitask.

MATT'S THOUGHTS

I asked Matt to give me his definition of multitasking and his use of this example. Given his experience in customer service, there were times when he needed to stock the shelves with products. Inevitably, customers would see him and ask questions. Matt might be able to answer some basic requests and still put up merchandise, but if he really wanted to give that customer the attention they deserved, he needed to stop what he was doing and focus on them.

"The ability to multitask might seem important, but I think that people don't recognize (me included), you can't really effectively multitask and get anything done efficiently. I thought I could do that when I was younger but not really now," Matt emphasized.

About as much multitasking Matt will do at this point is to recognize there are other issues he needs to address. If he is a passive participant, Matt may do two things at once (watch a webinar and do laundry—yes, that is true). When he becomes an active participant, full focus is given to what is in front of him.

TASK ADMINISTRATION

Task administration can seem pretty dry. While time optimization might not be at all spicy, managing your tasks is not very sexy but certainly necessary. It incorporates all aspects of the view of time we introduced at the beginning of the book.

As mentioned and implied throughout this chapter, time-optimized task design uses all the functions of time in the application of PEC (see Figure 1:1). There are single, functional tasks that are linear. Re-planned ones are started, sent back to the beginning, reworked, and then completed, having become variations of their original selves. Repeating tasks are done, then done again, and so on until their end date is met—cycles of continuous work. All are integrated options and examples of time that paint a picture of optimization.

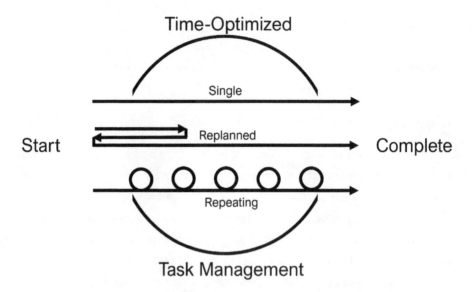

FIGURE 4:11 TASK TYPES MAKING UP TIME-OPTIMIZED TASK MANAGEMENT

Tasks that are time-optimized are not multitasked. There is an acknowledgment that attention is best placed on one item at a time. If you decide to have more than one detail open at the same time, attention will still be placed in one area, micro-tasking back and forth while concentrating on just one thing at a time.

CHAPTER 5

Time-Optimized Internal Focus

Discipline is kind of a dirty word in our culture to some degree.
It is my conviction and judgment that if you want to be focused, organized,
have boundaries, and be efficient, you are going to have to be disciplined.
The only one who is going to build that discipline is yourself.
(Rev. Dr. Hunter Camp)

I liked to draw for fun as a kid. I was not particularly good; I just had a good time doing the activity. As I got older and more "important" things took precedent, it faded from my conscious, and I never really thought about it or did anything to continue.

One Christmas, we (really, my wife) picked out and gave to our oldest son a book on how to draw. It was filled with projects, like how to draw bugs, dinosaurs, animals, and even cartoon characters. Everything that might catch a little boy's attention. Each illustration was followed by a series of instructions on what you needed to do to make your version.

One day, my son came up to me with the book and said, "Dad, do you want to draw with me?" I immediately made up some lame excuse about needing to watch this important football game on TV. That was when I felt "the look." For any man who has been married for any length of time (pun intended again), you can sense when your wife is giving you "the look." Even if you are not in the same room, to borrow a *Star Wars* term, you "sense a disturbance in the force." I looked up to see my lovely bride Susan staring me down, eyes darting from me to the dining room table. Like a Jedi mind trick, I was forced to comply (grumbling to myself the entire way).

Kenneth and I spent half the day at the table and had a blast. I rekindled an old desire, and my self-esteem was really helped along when K-Man would look over my shoulder and say, "Dad, that's really good!" We drew a variety of bugs, and we capped it off by each drawing a Tyrannosaurus rex. In the coming years, that led to me to create a variety of ink drawings (using the stippling method—a very forgiving technique) that usually became gifts to family members or friends.

As I write this today, it has probably been four years since my last completed sketch. It is not that I have lost the joy again; it is that it takes a lot of *internal* focus. As my story shows, I need to be more motivated to draw. When there is no inspiration, there is no progress or desire. I have probably started and stopped a dozen illustrations, possibly never to be finished. I kept delaying devoting the time, and after dawdling enough, the drawing stopped. To be committed, I also have to block out all diversions. Letting my guard down meant I let myself be unproductive.

To all the true artists out there who continuously create, bravo! You have mastered the internal focus to stay at it. For the rest of us, in this chapter, we will highlight how that applies *to time-optimized time management* in three areas.

By better understanding *procrastination,* we will see how you can set a plan to recognize and overcome stalling and postponement. *Motivation* (really, positive motivation) provides the concentrated brain power to keep your project or task on track. Then, we shift to *distractions* and the ways in which they hurt focus. Because it is time-optimized, we will weave in PEC and check-in on the underpinnings of time application.

A TIME-OPTIMIZED INTERNALLY FOCUSED PERSON—HUNTER CAMP

The Rev. Dr. Hunter Camp is my pastor. As a senior minister of a large and grow-ing church, he is extremely busy. I wanted to interview Hunter for this part of the book because he has so often demonstrated the ability to be ultra-focused.

It started with the first worship service I ever attended at Memorial Presbyte-rian Church, which is now my home church. As I walked down the aisle to receive communion, Hunter treated each congregant as if they were the only person in the room. Having never met me before, as I took the wafer and looked up, his gaze locked on mine, and he said, "Brother, the body of Christ, broken for you." It was like he had known me for years. I sat down and watched the rest approach. Hunter maintained that same focus and attention with every single worshipper.

Pastor Camp is an active person in his fifties, who looks much younger than that. Part of it is just his healthy approach to life, but it's also his love of surfing, photography, and writing. As of this writing, Hunter had his first book published called *The Glide: Confessions of a Florida Surfer*. Obviously, it is around surfing but also delves into a lot of his personal journey, reflection on God, the journey of life, and all the varied emotions that come with that.

As the pastoral head of staff of his second church, Hunter has had to learn to not only manage but to optimize his time. Readily available when needed, he has also established clear delineations between ministry and personal life. This disci-pline is tied to his strength to stay focused and not let internal attention waiver on what he has planned. I think this allows Hunter to have the energy to center himself on his work and his congregation.

As much as Hunter displays an intense internal focus, it is not at the expense of not wanting to learn. My pastor has a focused curiosity that drives self-im-provement. As we hear from Hunter throughout the chapter, you'll see things to emulate in your own time-optimized, internally focused plan.

PROCRASTINATION

There are a variety of reasons we delay. It can be a single cause or a combination of factors. Hence, many people do not stop to get to the root cause of the post-ponement but simply continue to defer the problem or opportunity, creating a cycle of procrastination.

Again, referring to the hundreds of Time Management Analysis (TMA) reports, 40 percent of the participants struggle with procrastination most or all of the time! A whopping 54 percent battle some or a little of the time, and only 6 percent have no issue at all with deferring projects, tasks, or assignments. At some point, you are going to get stuck.

Back in Chapter 3, when we were talking about the importance of completing assignments, I spoke about how I procrastinated on a project during a retail management training apprenticeship. My delay postponed my first department promotion out of the program. You'd think that would have cured me of my problem. That would be a big *nope*. Although, I do know how to recognize my issues better. It gets tied back to PEC. This challenge is one you need to take personally.

PERSONAL: IT IS ABOUT YOU

Many times, what can get overlooked is how you feel: emotionally, physically, and spiritually. Do not think about discounting this, particularly if you procrastinate on more than one thing.

> *Evidence suggests that putting off important tasks causes stress, and this additional stress contributes to negative psychophysiological impacts on the body which increase our vulnerability for illness. Previous research has linked chronic procrastination to a range of stress-related health problems such as headaches, digestive issues, colds and flus, and insomnia.*[1]

Anxiety can cause you to falter. Depression will have a detrimental effect. A need to be perfect and look perfect will cause you to hesitate. Little or no self-control raids you of time-optimized thoughtfulness. A look at yourself first may be just the ticket and makes the rest of the ride easier.

PERSONAL: PREPARATION

After eliminating or recognizing any bodily impediments, dive into PEC. Again, the difference here is to proverbially look in the mirror and own that these are *your* issues and not to blame others or look for alternatives. Instances of stalling can come because there is not enough detailed provision on the front end. We have already gone into preparation details of general planning in Chapter 3 and task administration in Chapter 4. We'll get into organization and personal care later.

Should you be a part of the 40 percent on the TMA that constantly battle procrastination, as you plan, you must ask and challenge yourself on the following:

- Have I clearly defined the goals *for me?*
- Do I have everything sequenced correctly *for me?*
- Am I confident I will meet the expectations I have set *for myself?*

If this sounds selfish, that is the point. Make this process all about you. Ultimately, what you do will impact others. Therefore, while self-centered in nature, your ability to positively answer the three questions will reduce the negative impact you will have on others.

Step back and view at a high-level the activity causing the slowdown. A short but comprehensive take on procrastination is the book titled *Eat that Frog*. Brian Tracy encourages, "One of the best ways to overcome procrastination is for you to get your mind off the huge task in front of you and focus on a single action you can take."[2] Small steps are a great way to provide the emotional boost you need to show progress.

A mentor and friend told me many times, "Never fail to state the obvious." To honor that, please—set solid deadlines, get over any task aversion, and get to know your time commitment.

PERSONAL: EXECUTION

Good. You planned well. The earlier topics you have read in this book have changed your life! Happily, you dive into the task or project you have developed and then . . . you . . . seem . . . to . . . not . . . make . . . progress. Yeah, I was probably a little too full of myself there about the book so far.

Let's bring some reality back. "Procrastination isn't a unique character flaw or a mysterious curse on your ability to manage time, but a way of coping with challenging emotions and negative moods induced by certain tasks—boredom, anxiety, insecurity, frustration, resentment, self-doubt and beyond."[3]

This is a good time to bring in our definition again.

> *Time-optimized time management* is a continuous pursuit of the **right preparation**, along with the **right execution**, to escalate **broad control** over personal productivity.

Preparation, execution, and control work together, and the work is unceasing. As the emotional impact creeps back in, watch for the following signs:

- There are no immediate results to show progress, so you begin to wonder if you should continue or stop.
- Other priorities have created time constraints from your original plan.
- Expectations have changed, and you are frustrated and don't want to go back to the preparation phase.
- You thought you should be done at this point, and there is now more to do.

When here, you come back to the questions noted in the preparation area and ask them again—but with a slight twist.

- How are the goals achievable *for me?*
- How has the sequence of events changed *for me?*
- Why am I not confident that I will meet the expectations I have set *for myself?*

Notice how the questions are now open-ended, reflective of the continuous pursuit of the right execution. After answering candidly to yourself, this should affirm the direction you need to take forward to completion or to alter or fine-tune.

PERSONAL: CONTROL

An aspect of procrastination that differs from other time-optimized challenges (like external focus issues, to be discussed in the next chapter) is you are always in control. Stop scratching your head in confusion or annoyance. As I have been saying, procrastination is about *you*. It is your choice to move forward or delay, step it up or stay in place, drive ahead or park it.

The passive control of procrastination happens when you choose to ignore and not follow the time-optimized definition, particularly the three words of *escalate broad control*. Preferring inaction to action is in your control and should you choose to exercise that, you delay and narrow command over the task or project.

Using the pattern of *P* and *E*, we adjust the questions a third time for *E*.

* What needs to change for the goals to be achievable *for me?*
* What do I need to change in the sequence of events *for me?*
* What must I do to be more confident in meeting the expectations I have set *for myself?*

Again, these questions are open-ended and tie back to continuously escalating a broad sense of control back into the activity.

"Me Questions" of Procrastination PEC			
Trait	*Preparation*	*Execution*	*Control*
Goals	Clearly defined?	Achievable?	Change?
Sequence	Set correctly?	Anything changed?	Change?
Expectations	Confident to complete?	Still confident?	Change?

FIGURE 5:1 THE PEC MATRIX OF OVERCOMING PROCRASTINATION

Figure 5:1 summarizes what we have just been discussing. In each segment of PEC, you must overcome impediments to avoid procrastination, and you may have to answer questions more than once. *Preparation* is an internal gut check to give you the confidence to move forward. *Execution* makes you monitor your work to challenge yourself based on your planning. Finally, *control* is simply questioning the need to change. A "no" means you proceed and progress; a "yes" is on you to adjust and then progress.

DECISION FATIGUE

The very nature of PEC is about constant action and will involve a lot of decision-making. That can be energizing when you show and make progress. It can be frustrating and feed the procrastination sloth if you don't see forward movement.

I recognize that is a risk, particularly if you choose to use the information in this section and still seem hindered in your productivity advancement.

The American Medical Association defines *decision fatigue* for us.

> *Making decisions day in and day out—whether they are as easy picking a route home from work or as difficult as navigating a once-in-a-lifetime pandemic—can be exhausting and cause people to feel overwhelmed, anxious or stressed. This is known as decision fatigue, which is a state of mental overload that can impede a person's ability to continue making decisions. You have probably experienced decision fatigue during the pandemic because it has added new layers of complexity to the daily choices we are confronted with.*[4]

Some of the side effects of decision fatigue are impulsivity, avoidance, and indecision.

I do not know how many times I have started a project and then recklessly changed directions. Many times, it is to do something else that might be productive, but I do not do what was intended to be a higher priority. I also dodge, making excuses or blaming someone else for interrupting my concentration. I hesitate, falsely putting myself back in preparation only, not using execution and control.

There is some debate in the medical community about the validity of decision fatigue as a medical condition. Not being in the field, I can't answer that. Having a passion for productivity, I am going to go out on a limb to say it does impact your time optimization. If your brain is in a fog as you try to answer the questions I posed previously, take a break. Then, after you take a break, go to Chapter 8 and review your personal care. You may need to address giving your body, mind, and spirit some much needed rest to come back and tackle your situation with the right mindset.

HUNTER'S VIEW

One of the first questions I asked Hunter was, "Given your occupation (as a minister) how do you stay successful in not becoming a procrastinator?"

With no delay whatsoever, he answered, "I think that is a question I am still trying to unpack."

As he continues to seek to deliver well, he has "four legs of the table" to support his efforts, and they are focus, organization, boundaries, and efficiencies. These attributes play off each other. We address his four aspects to some degree at some point in the book. Peeking a little into Chapter 10, Hunter's procrastination approach is, in part, an outline of his time-optimized life.

Hunter wanted to make a point that he feels it is normal and acceptable to procrastinate. Now, before you curse me for having to read this section, he distinguishes that "between low- and high-value items." You can learn to differentiate between the two through organization and establishing boundaries.

We also explored the ability to be self-aware of your actions as a catalyst to recognizing when procrastination creeps into daily life. Hunter solves this through one of our personal care items to be discussed in Chapter 8, that is, to take a formal break. For Dr. Camp, that means leaving his desk and going for a ten-minute walk with the purpose of clearing his mind to come back and engage fully in the activity at hand. This is a clear example of inventing time to create time.

Finally, Hunter is a goal-oriented person. Goals help motivate and drive him to results. However, he has recognized that sometimes not spending enough time in the process can allow for procrastination to seep in on execution. Therefore, he appreciates the investment of time at the front end more.

MOTIVATION

Motivation and procrastination go hand in hand. Usually, if you are positively motivated, there is a drive and determination that crowds out procrastination. Likewise, when you are procrastinating, there will be some elements of being negatively motivated in the mix. Therefore, the motivation you need to tap into when there is a loss of internal focus should provide incentive and inspiration and cause you to step forward.

You might say (and you would be correct) there is an entire industry created around motivating you. Millions follow personalities like Tony Robbins, Arianna Huffington, Nick Vujicic, Chris Gardner, and Gary Vaynerchuk and rely on their advice to spark an internal fire of personal enthusiasm.[6] You might also ask, "Then isn't that external and not internal?"

I would happily answer, "Correct you are!" Getting peripheral help is external, and I fully support that. Yet the desire to change must initiate from the inside, from you to yourself. In addition, when it comes to *time optimization* and focus, motivation must originate from within.

The website *HR for Health* released an article in which the author notes five ways to motivate employees in the context of the health industry (and we want all medical personnel to be positively motivated when they care for us). The methods consisted of showing trust, giving purpose, concentrating on training and growth, creating a healthy and pleasant environment, and recognizing achievements.[7] I can get onboard with all of those in a place I work. There is also no reason for you not to turn that around and point those same ways to motivate at you. Let's also add once again . . . PEC.

MOTIVATION: PREPARATION

When lacking motivation on an assignment, prepare to reignite your mind by asking yourself some basic questions that again focus on you.

- Do I trust *myself* to get this done?
- Is the purpose clearly defined *for me*?
- Does there need to be more analysis *for me* to move forward?
- Is the environment right *for me* to work?
- Have I thought about the benefits of achievement *for me*?

I readily admit, there is a risk for you to repeatedly answer no and use the negative answers as excuses to procrastinate. Use the five questions to break the emotional impasse, not as a justification to stay in place.

MOTIVATION: EXECUTION

You have taken a step and prepared. The motivation juices are flowing. Progress begins, but then life intrudes again. You find you are stumbling, and the enthusiasm is just not there. That happens, trust me. I could fill this book with example after example of the times I started out excited and quickly lost incentive. Here again, we go back to the five questions and reaffirm our commitment by adding one word: *still*.

- Do I *still* trust *myself* to get this done?
- Is the purpose *still* clearly defined *for me*?
- Does there *still* need to be more analysis *for me* to move forward?
- Is the environment *still* right *for me* to work?
- Have I *still* thought about the benefits of achievement *for me*?

The *still* is not an adjective like motionless, immobile, or unmoving. It is an adverb like in spite of everything, yet, or even now. There is a relationship of action to this period of PEC. If one or more of the answers is *no*, then jump back to the preparation part to see if things need to change to get back the forward motivation. Should priorities change, that might change the urgency of your reason and purpose for the activity.

MOTIVATION: CONTROL

Knowing I am repeating myself, I remind you again that PEC is a three-way relationship. Should you find yourself in a motivation feedback loop, pinging between preparation and execution, you need to assert *control*. Like we did in procrastination, we insert *change* into the mix.

- What needs to *change* for me to trust *myself* to get this done?
- Has the purpose *changed for me*?
- Do I need to *change* how I am analyzing this *for me* to move forward?
- Do I need to *change* the environment *for me* to work?
- Do I need to *change* how I have thought about the benefits of achievement *for me*?

Change can bring pressure. Your choice can be to embrace that pressure to push you forward or let the pressure stop you and keep you in place. Brian Tracy notes, "To reach your full potential, you must form the habit of putting the pressure on yourself and not waiting for someone to come along and do it for you."[8] While he does apply that to procrastination, it works just as well here for motivation.

"Me Questions" for Motivation			
Trait	*Preparation*	*Execution*	*Control*
Trust	Do you really?	Confident?	Change?
Purpose	Clearly defined?	Rationale holds?	Change?
Analysis	Additional work?	Examined right?	Change?
Environment	Right setting?	Best conditions?	Change?
Benefits	Correctly defined?	Advantageous and valuable?	Change?

FIGURE 5:2 THE PEC MATRIX OF STAYING POSITIVELY MOTIVATED

If you complete an honest evaluation of motivational PEC, answering no to any of the questions in Figure 5:2, preparation, execution, and control should not negatively impact your motivation. Time-optimized time management is a continuous process, and if you find your motivation is misplaced in a task or project that must be altered, delayed, or even canceled, it just means you get to fill that space with something that feeds you back into a positive motivational mindset.

HUNTER'S APPROACH

In the course of his day as a pastor, Hunter can see all kinds of events take place that run a full range of emotion, from celebration to tragedy. Because of that, positive motivation for him is a constant and never-ending process.

Hunter does not like things hanging over his head and is committed to finishing tasks and activities to allow the freedom to address pastoral concerns and events that arise. "I like to have free time to be able to surf, hang out at the beach, spend time with my family. To do that, I must knock things out so that I have more free time." That incentive keeps him in a constructive motivational state.

Because Dr. Camp has an earned persona of being focused and motivated, I asked him, "If you weren't as motivated as you are now, what would life be like?"

With a look of some discomfort, he responded, "Well, I think I'd be drowning. I don't think someone can do my particular vocation and my particular role and have a life outside of the church if they are not focused and committed. So, if I don't stay committed [to a life outside the church], then I would drown. Knowing my own capacity, I would have gotten burnt out and left the church and ministry a long time ago."

Finally, the common theme for Hunter (which is why he was a great interviewee for this section) is staying focused on the work at hand and not trying to juggle too many things at once. This causes you to be overwhelmed, and it is hard to stay motivated and effective.

DISTRACTIONS

If you remember back in Chapter 2, I risked my marriage by explaining the difference between my clean and organized desk and the system Susan has of keeping just about everything in plain sight. I only mention that again, because I am going to use another workplace example, and I want to make it clear; the person being mentioned here is not my wife.

Now that I have that qualified . . . I was working with a client who struggles with distractions. Internal challenges that impede progress. She asked me if I could look at her office to see if there was anything I saw that could be changed to help her stay focused. As you know, I am a firm believer in organization and that everything has a space and place. Upon entering, I noticed stacks of papers, books, Post-it notes, memo pads, legal pads, and periodicals.

I asked her how she felt about the space. "It is a distraction to me. I know I need to file the papers and get things straightened out. I was going to come in on my day off to try [to] do that, but I always seem to have other things that take priority." I can relate.

Going back to my wife, her desk looks familiar to my client's workspace—except to my wife, it is not a distraction. She can be productive for long stretches. Like my client, I would find it very hard to work in the clutter and would become unfocused and sidetracked by the situation. Unlike me, my client is not as neurotic. Given her days can be unpredictable, having a neat office area has not risen to the level that overrides other things that continuously have significance.

While my long-term answer was to tell her she needs to invest the time to organize her space if it continues to cause her distraction, in the short-term, I took a large empty box, and we neatly stacked everything into it and set it off in the corner. I told her, "Your desk is clean. You have found a way to remove the distraction. How do you feel?"

With a smile on her face, she said, "This will work!"

I emphasized this solution was only when she needed to complete deeper and more focused work. Ultimately, she was required to figure out a permanent and lasting answer (to which we talked about organization). What my client's example shows is that distractions are like a series of eliminations you want to remove to focus, lower to concentrate, and diminish to be attentive.

Cal Newport references distractions and the fallacy of easy resolutions in a variety of places in his book *Deep Work*.

> In my experience, it's common to treat undistracted concentration as a habit like flossing—something that you know how to do and know is good for you, but that you've been neglecting due to lack of motivation. This mind-set is appealing because it implies you can transform your working life from distracted to focused overnight if you simply muster enough motivation. But this understanding ignores the difficulty of focus and the hours necessary to strengthen your "mental muscle."

While I provided a quick and temporary solution for my client, it was not meant to be a long-term solution. We had a conversation on a permanent approach that would require much more sustained effort.

Like we have done with procrastination and motivation, PEC will be used for a time-optimized approach to overcome internal disturbances. Before we plunge into the details, I need to talk more about the types of distractions impacting our ability to be time-optimized.

- *Electronic distractions* are a category on its own because of the addictive nature that is presented to us. Limiting internet browsing, checking email, regulating texts, restraining social media engagement, and quarantining the smartphone (which is the root cause of the electronic problem for many) prevents us from being sucked into a void of time worthlessness.

- *Personal distractions* highlight many things tied to healthy actions and needs like sleep, thirst, breaks, clutter, hunger, anxiety, and general laziness.
- *Professional distractions* revolve around the demands of your job. It is easy to get drawn into things like office politics, gossip, noisy coworkers and a loud office environment, faulty equipment, micro-management (leader or subordinate), too many meetings, and a toxic workplace.

Yes, again I do see it; some of these could be considered external factors beyond your control, particularly under the professional group. I'll give you that, but if they are truly distractions for you, an internal challenge for mastery, you own taking the steps to make a change. Chances are, those around you may not even be aware it is an issue for you because of the internal nature of the challenge.

Here we go again with PEC.

DISTRACTION: PREPARATION

In college, distractions owned my study process (or lack thereof). Typically, I started in my dorm room. My roommate would come in, and I would stop and talk. I would hear something in the hall, so I needed to investigate. Seeking quiet, I would go to the library. I would pick a spot in a high-traffic area. Wait! *There is a friend I need to talk to.* Then it was time to move to a more isolated location. Before I got into any groove, it would be a couple of hours wasted by distractions.

As has been the pattern in this chapter, preparing for a time-optimized activity to limit distractions, there are questions you need to ask yourself.

- Do I need to address or prepare for any personal care needs like sleep, hunger, thirst, and energy?
- Do I need to spend time organizing the space around me, removing obstacles that keep me from being focused?
- Do I need to change location?

- Do I need to feed any social media urges?
- Do I need to answer any texts or emails?
- Do I need to have my phone on and available during this time?

Preparation starts with the physical and mental state and ends with limiting or blocking access to things like your phone or electronics. You are attempting to isolate yourself both inside and out.

DISTRACTION: EXECUTION

Distractions can be a battle of will. It is a struggle I constantly fight. Therefore, the *execution* part of distraction PEC lies in the *recognition* that you have been taken off course, your purpose is not being fulfilled, and your productivity has come to a screeching halt. As a result, the preparation questions now adjust to perception challenges of your current state of progress.

- Are my personal care needs causing me to be distracted (sleep, hunger, thirst, and energy)?
- Is the space around me causing me to be distracted?
- Is the location causing me to be distracted?
- Is social media causing me to be distracted?
- Are texts and emails causing me to be distracted?
- Is my phone causing me to be distracted?

The execution *against* distraction is an acknowledgment of a stoppage in work. However, I do not want you to jump right back into the preparation phase. That might need to be done, but first, you must strongly and quickly move to try to assert control.

DISTRACTION: CONTROL

Going back to my poor study habits, you'll notice my response to every distraction was to change something. As we have talked much during this book, I was reacting to circumstances, not proactively seeking to set myself up for success. Accordingly, distraction *control* is first an attempt to reassert your will back into your work, then to address more *preparation*—only if you find *execution* is beyond your grasp.

- Am I able to wait and address my personal care needs later (sleep, hunger, thirst, and energy)?
- Am I able to overlook the space around me to keep going?
- Am I able to stay in this location to finish?
- Am I able to ignore social media to focus?
- Am I able to wait on any texts and emails to get done?
- Am I able to shut off my phone to fully work?

These control trigger questions are designed to get you back on track and not take you backward. Having said that, PEC is a continuous process, and if you need to go back to preparation to better execute and control the outcome, do so without shame or defeat. You are learning in the process.

I have mentioned before, the PEC relationship of time optimization is shown as an equilateral triangle. With distractions, there is still a relationship, but control has more emphasis. (See Figure 5:3)

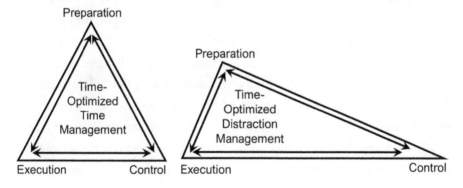

FIGURE 5:3 OVERALL TIME OPTIMIZATION COMPARED TO DISTRACTION TIME OPTIMIZATION

If you find you are constantly distracted, even after following the PEC process, pay close attention to the planning and task design phases. Therein lies the opening for distractions to take hold. If goals are not properly established, distraction lurks. There is not enough time allocated; distraction awaits. You are working outside of peak productive times; distraction pops up. You have not prioritized correctly; distraction is around the corner.

"Me Questions" of Distractions			
Trait	*Preparation*	*Execution*	*Control*
Personal Care	Address any issues?	Is this a cause?	Can I wait?
Space	Organize area?	Is this a cause?	Can I overlook?
Location	Change current?	Is this a cause?	Can I stay?
Social Media	Spend time before?	Is this a cause?	Can I ignore?
Emails/Texts	Answer now?	Is this a cause?	Can I wait?
Phone	Needed?	Is this a cause?	Can I shut off?

FIGURE 5:4 THE PEC MATRIX OF MANAGING DISTRACTIONS

HUNTER'S MANNER

As a pastor of a large and growing church, the demands on Dr. Camp's time can be never-ending. Because focus is crucial to him, he pays close attention to the surrounding environment.

Having been in his office and seeing it through the computer screen, I can attest that it is organized. "In my study, my desk and the space around me is pretty sparse, and by that, I mean there is not a lot going on. I have a small desk, and the only things on it are items I know what to do with . . . they have a purpose." Dr. Camp is very diligent to not allow items into his workspace that are going to distract him.

Like procrastination, Hunter feels it is suitable and forgiving to be distracted when your high-value tasks have been completed. He does not feel distractions in themselves are a problem for productivity; rather, it is allowing too many distractions to keep you from or take you away from the work that needs to get done.

Another approach of Hunter's is to allow those distractions in and attend to them in unexpected moments of free time. "If I have five minutes before the next meeting, what is the best use of my time? It is in these moments that I will allow myself to be distracted by watching a surf video."

In his mind, an allowance of a small distraction after finishing a large project is, "fine and dandy—it is like a mini-vacation." However, Hunter emphasized you need to have good boundaries around those mini-vacations you might take during the day.

Lastly, Hunter sees how discipline and distraction are tied together. *"Discipline* is kind of a dirty word in our culture to some degree. It is my conviction and judgment that if you want to be focused, organized, have boundaries, and be efficient, you are going to have to be disciplined. The only one who is going to build in that discipline is yourself."

Very fitting, given the internal focus concept that are distractions.

INSIDE OUT

Chapter 5 was all about you. Time-optimized internal focus looks inward.

Someone else can't procrastinate for you. They may influence your inaction, but you choose to maintain in your current spot. You may ask for outside help (totally appropriate), but the change starts with your *ask*. External events may extinguish a spark, but you still need to decide to end the delay.

Motivation by itself can reverse, keep, or propel productivity momentum. Time-optimized motivation is positive but realistic. PEC will keep you grounded by being inspired and determined to maintain the flow of efficiency in the right direction.

Many distractions are triggered by our senses. That may make it easy to blame our environment or surroundings. Fair enough, but unlike interruptions (which we discuss in the next chapter), these are internal, controllable actions that take discipline to get to time optimization.

Successful internal focus can be *time viewed* differently, depending on your individual circumstance. It could be linear, needing a nudge from you to move forward. It could be cyclical, making you look backward to change current behavior to move forward. Your productivity might be an illusion, wishing for movement but not seeing the results. If anything, I hope this chapter has shown you that you have the inward ability to optimize your time management.

CHAPTER 6

Time-Optimized External Focus

Success for me has always been about spending every second
of my life meaningfully. If I am going to be doing something,
I have to be 100 percent in it and focused.
(Dr. Divya Jaitly)

T he last chapter was all about you. This chapter is all about everyone else and the peripheral or outer happenings that cause us to lose focus. Time-optimized external focus takes the outside in, challenging you to be negative in preparation, execution, and control. Having said that, there is one huge *but* in the PEC of outward emphasis. This is not permission for you to be negatively negative. I don't want angry emails and letters saying I encouraged unenthusiastic and harmful behavior. This is an opportunity for you to *not say yes* to everything that leads to the detriment of your productivity. However, as I mentioned way back in Chapter 2, "but do this with gentleness and respect."[1]

For years, I said yes to everything. Attend a meeting? I am there. Write a report? I am on it. Analyze data? The spreadsheet is open. Whatever was asked, to use an analogy from a coworker, "You are like a golden retriever; someone throws the ball, and you go fetch it. They keep throwing it, and you keep bringing it back to them." Unlike a golden, there would come a point where I did not do it joyfully. I became resentful, angry, and frustrated.

What was my problem? I did not want to be negative.

At some point, one more thing would be placed on my plate (no, we will not dive into the buffet analogy again), and I would fail at delivering on something I committed to in the first place. Up until that point, I usually worked too many hours, letting my personal life suffer. All to the point of not meeting expectations—my own or someone else's.

Because I was blessed with so many great bosses, instead of looking to punish me, there would be questions like, "Why didn't you tell me?" What followed would be a review of what my to-do list looked like, with a re-prioritization of activities to bring productivity back to reality and time to better optimization.

Let's see how being externally focused ties into the old saying *less is more* by using PEC.

A TIME-OPTIMIZED EXTERNALLY FOCUSED PERSON—DIVYA JAITLY

I have known Dr. Divya Jaitly for several years.

Through LinkedIn, she invited me to participate as a panelist in one of her leadership masterclasses. From there, it led to a strategic partnership agreement between our two companies. I find that amazing because our connection has only been through electronic measures. We have yet to meet face to face. Even through these limited means and separated by oceans and continents (she in India, me in the United States), I knew early in our interactions that she was a decisive person.

Divya attributes her focus to a father with a career in the military and an academic mother. That led her to become a self-described "jack-of-all-trades." The result of that focus has been an incredible journey from being crowned as a Miss India finalist and model, to a Doctorate in Organizational Leadership, and now owning her third business as a successful entrepreneur.

She credits her father for imparting upon her the importance of time and contingencies—two aspects that must be considered together to be successful at time management. She states, "Time is more valuable than money; the money will follow."

Where I really got to experience her focus firsthand was during a meeting I had with her over the Time Management Analysis (TMA) tool I have mentioned. I was in the testing phase and asked her if she and her team would mind taking the TMA so I could test the algorithms and format. She graciously accepted. As I was reviewing the data and my analysis with her, I felt I was not making a compelling case. I stopped the presentation and asked her about her thoughts.

Divya declared, "The tool is fine. Now I want you to develop a leadership one for me."

"I'm not planning on making a leadership tool."

What followed was a lively discussion and a proposal from her on the merits and opportunity of such an endeavor. She was focused and targeted. I remember walking out of my office after we were done and my wife asking, "So how did it go?"

With somewhat of a perplexed look on my face, I said, "I think I am building a new tool."

From that initial meeting, we have since developed two additional instruments called The Leadership Assessment Tool (LAT) and the Public Speaking Assessment Tool (PSAT). Both were a quick and productive process. We limited our interruptions of each other. We talked only when needed and always put the goals in context. While you might say I did not do a good job of "saying no" on the front end, we honored and respected each other's perspective that we could say no when needed as the tools were being built.

Dr. Divya's diverse professional journey has helped her "create my own niche across industries and I come with a unique perspective from media, entertainment, learning and development, education, as well as hardcore business consulting." These transferrable skills serve her well and could not have been possible unless Divya was extremely focused, and that is why I have asked for her perspective, which you will find throughout this chapter.

TALKING TOO MUCH

Talking too much in a time-optimized sense is not about small talk. "Small talk [is] defined as polite, light-hearted and superficial exchanges that are non-work related—greetings, farewells or superficial chat about how your day is going."[2]

To be time efficient does not mean you stop all communication, bury your head, and get your tasks done. Human interaction, on both a professional and a personal level, has many beneficial qualities. Where I seek to interrupt (which we'll discuss in a bit) is when talking stops the time of progress.

This concept of talking tied to time management can really straddle the internal and external aspects of focus. I could have easily placed this subject in the last chapter, but I felt it best to count it as an external issue. Yes, you can and should discipline your speech when it gets in the way of efficiency. However, it becomes more difficult when someone else's conversation, dialog, and chatter become your problem.

This is particularly challenging on the job. "Talking in the workplace is a hot-button issue. Too much talking can lead to a slump in productivity, while cracking down on conversations can lead to poor morale among employees."[3]

In the course of my career, there have been countless reasons I found myself in situations of all talk and no action.

- ✓ There were no clear goals established.
- ✓ The activity or project is hard.
- ✓ Others seek affirmation from you.
- ✓ Everything needs to be perfect before something is undertaken.
- ✓ There is a fear of moving forward.
- ✓ There is a fear of failure.

In all these examples, this can be someone else, or this could be you. Either way, something is not getting done that needs to be done.

Referencing our time-optimized definition of being *a continuous pursuit of the right* preparation, *along with the right* execution, *to escalate broad* control *over personal productivity*, we will provide options to govern discussion and regulate the external impact it has on your pursuit of higher productivity.

TALK CHECK-IN: PREPARATION

So far, you have heard the phrase *proactive versus reactive* used quite a bit in this book. Trying to anticipate any future challenges is a good investment of time. This is very appropriate when the issue of talking encumbers work. Therefore, I have adopted the principles outlined in the Daily Check-in Meeting as described by Patrick Lencioni in his book *Death by Meeting*.

> *The purpose of the Daily Check-in is to help team members avoid confusion about priorities and are translated into action on a regular basis. It provides a quick forum for ensuring that nothing falls through the cracks on a given day and that no one steps on anyone else's toes. Just as important, it helps eliminate the need for unnecessary and time-consuming email chains about schedule coordination.*[4]

Lencioni challenges the participants to hold the gathering for five minutes at most, making it consistent by doing them each workday.

The context for time optimization is a little different since the example I used from *Death by Meeting* is specifically about . . . well, meetings. However, it is a great parallel to ask yourself these questions to create boundaries by having a brief conversation with other potential talk disruptors. Let's call these the *Talk Check-in questions*.

- Who must I preemptively talk to today?
- What are going to be their concerns?
- How can I help them?
- Will it require additional time?
- What needs to happen for progress to continue?

This does not need to be daily; these are targeted individuals who will seek to take away your time with their concerns (many legitimate). Remember, you are in the preparation phase for any Talk Check-ins. There might be many days where this is not even on your radar. However, you want your radar on, always scanning for talk blips on the horizon.

TALK CHECK-IN: EXECUTION

When I worked for a small company, every day I took what was called the "good morning walk." I started at the front of the building and strolled through each department, saying, "Good morning" to every associate. It became a game for some. In the customer service department, it turned out to be modified, and I would say, "Good morning, angels."

To which they would respond, "Good morning, Charlie." I would like to note here; they started the term, not me, and I was not violating any HR boundaries. Also, if you have no idea what I am talking about, search the term "Charlie's Angels," and you will find a television show and movie references to give context.

Back to reality. The purpose of the good morning walk was to show appreciation and acknowledge the employees, but it was also a chance for me to execute any Talk Check-ins with specific people or department heads. While I did not ask the formal questions within this process that have been created for this book, it was an opportunity for me to pre-address any issues or challenges from others to save the talking that might come later.

While you can approach the Talk Check-in a variety of ways, remember: you want to keep it short. Whether it is done in a *Daily Check-in* or a *good morning walk*, this is a proactive way to optimize your time.

Your execution questions become:

- Have I preemptively talked to everyone on my list?
- What are their actual concerns?
- Was I able to help them?
- Will it require more time and did a formal time to discuss get set?
- Did I emphasize what progress needs to be made?

In these *moments* (I use that word intentionally, I don't want you to convey to the other parties that this is a meeting), show a sense of urgency, quickness, the need to move on, and the informal nature of the discussion. You may have some structured purposes, but your goal is to use a small amount of time now to keep them from taking up more of your minutes later.

TALK CHECK-IN: CONTROL

Talk Check-in control is all about time, *limited* time. I know—another obvious statement. However, this is not meant to be a formal placeholder on your calendar. It is meant as a selective time-management tool you use preemptively, targeted to prevent unnecessary talk or wasted conversation tied to unmet goals or fear of execution.

My good morning walk lasted all of ten minutes. I was able to build relationship capital and, at the same time, provide any clarity on items that might impact me. The result may well be another meeting added to my calendar, but that formality (and good time optimization) would lead to progress. With this, the questions of Talk Check-in PEC change.

- Am I keeping to my list, removing people, and do I need to add others?
- Do their actual concerns lead to progress and forward momentum?
- Did my help move things along?
- Have I identified what needs to be accomplished in any formal time that was created?
- Does the other person understand what progress needs to be made?

Unlike other elements of time optimization and the view of time perspectives we discussed in Chapter 1, control here is about being linear and quick with your methods. The goal is to simply prompt and prod for information. You do not want to use the Talk Check-in as a recurring feedback loop where you have a conversation every day about the same thing. Quite the opposite. You want to use this time to initiate action or change.

Talk Check-in Time Optimization			
Trait	*Preparation*	*Execution*	*Control*
People	Who?	All talked to?	Add, remove?
Concerns	What are they?	Are they the same?	Do they lead to progress?
Help	How?	Was I able?	Was progress made?
Identify	Additional time?	Require more time?	Formalized additional time?
Progress	How?	Emphasize progress?	Understanding of progress?

FIGURE 6:1 THE PEC OF PROACTIVELY REDUCING TIME WASTING TALK

At the beginning of the chapter, I challenged you to be negative (not negatively negative) in your external-focused approach. The Talk Check-in process may not look like it is negative. In fact, you will probably develop deeper relationships with the recipients of your attention. Nonetheless, a formal and impersonal nature can come across when you are brief and focused. This is not small talk, but it is also not casual conversation. It is warm but also a straight and undeviating time-optimized chat for you.

DIVYA'S LIMIT

I mentioned at the beginning of the chapter that Dr. Jaitly is from India. While this does not tie directly into this section, I just wanted to say that to my American ears, she has a cool accent. Because she coaches others on public speaking, Divya's choice of words is descriptive yet concise.

Because of her knowledge of communicating and coaching others (particularly business leaders) to present well, there is a method for investing the time to understand how one delivers their words and at what pace. She offered, "That input and insight should come from your cognitive ability that we all have, but we don't harness it and model the other persons or persons we are speaking to." The idea of modeling is a concept that reveals that as we spend time with people, we subconsciously pick up their traits and mannerisms. The key is to recognize that consciously to make a deeper connection with the other person or persons.

The other area of talking focus for Divya is content. By lacking the right content, she knows people will tend to overcompensate by talking too much—to try to get away with not having enough substance. Without paying attention to your nerves and anxiety, content, and delivery, Divya said, "It may make you have verbal diarrhea."

For this section, I took years of work by Dr. Divya and tried to summarize (albeit awkwardly) her approach to talk in a situation. The next step is to move the talk to action. I love her approach here too. "I have noticed that when people tend to talk a lot, a good way is to test and help them convert their thoughts into action. Find whether there is a bridge [for] the gap to give them or create a specific task and put it on paper."

This technique can be used in a variety of situations. If there is a lot of talking, ask the "talker" to write down their project or proposal, even if it is just in an email. As they work through that process, it will either solidify their approach or give them a focus to move from talk to action.

INTERRUPTIONS

Back in Chapter 3, I discussed my days in a retail management training program, and the challenge I had in completing a project, which caused me a delay in the placement of my first assignment. When I did get promoted, it was as a department manager for the men's clothing section of the store. If you have any experience *working retail* (as we called it), you know that interruptions are your life. Customers want attention, and they expect to get it.

In my role as a department manager, many times, I was out on the floor putting out product and straightening my area. When I needed to get merchandise from the stockroom, I would be peppered with multiple disturbances from customers needing help with a pant size, advice on shirt and tie combinations, or the location of particular merchandise. I am not going to lie; it could get really annoying. I know, that is not the right attitude—and one I look back on now and know I could have done better. After all, if it wasn't for the customers' buying, I would not need to stock the shelves.

My problem was not the customer; it was me. I did not know what PEC was back then, but I sure did not use it. I did not do any *preparation* for figuring out the best times, allocating the right times, and deciding what I wanted to get done. Since I had no plan, I could not *execute* it. There was no *control* because I was very ad hoc in my approach, which meant I was out on the floor when there were a lot of customers.

I am not going to provide you with a full-proof plan to save you from interruptions. For some of you, that might be the purpose of your job, to be interrupted. Leaders, in a desire to be accessible, should make allowances for unexpected breaks in activity.

PEC will aid in the anticipation of disruptions and make allowances for you to apply some *negative* (with gentleness and respect) solutions that keep you on track and time-optimized. As we discussed with distractions (internal disruptions), there are three categories of interruptions (external disruptions).

- *Planning interruptions* are a category that, because of a lack of provision (on your part or someone else's), you are being disturbed. Poor scheduling, no to-do list, no protected time, too much delegation, complex problems, time management, and no project ownership all open you up to getting "unwanted" visitors.
- *Surrounding interruptions* highlight many things tied to the work environment, family, coworkers, boss, meetings, location, breaks, and equipment.
- *Communication interruptions* revolve around the demands of your job. Things like phone calls, emails, corporate policies, training, experience, and texts.

If this looks familiar, well, it is. Head back to distractions in the last chapter, and you will see some common items. Remember, the key difference, though: you succumb to a distraction that affects your productivity, so you own it. An interruption intrudes from the outside and diminishes your time to maximize efficiency. Let's PEC our way through it.

One final note: After being a retail manager for a couple of years, I got transferred and promoted to another location (where I met my future wife, Susan). My new department was women's accessories, handbags, sleepwear, underwear, and bras. I quickly realized that I was never really bothered and was very productive with putting out merchandise. Few women asked me for advice or help. My interruptions were almost nonexistent.

INTERRUPTION: PREPARATION

Preparing for interruptions might seem like a contradiction in terms. If you set it up well enough, then there shouldn't be interruptions. Right? All true, but that is only part of the equation. Interruptions will come no matter how well you plan. The kind of preparation we are discussing here is also preparing yourself to be negative. You formulate a strategy that allows you to quickly place the burden back on the interrupter.

Based on this, there is a two-part nature of time-optimized interruption prevention. Here are the first set of questions to answer around the preparation of PEC. Typically, this is done at the beginning of the day and right before you embark on a focused task or project that requires minimal or no intrusions.

- Do I have my calendar blocked off for this time?
- Is this on my to-do list?
- Have I negotiated protected time for this?
- Have I informed the appropriate people about the need for protected time?
- Have I turned off the necessary electronic devices? *This will also help you with distractions as well.*
- Do I understand my alternatives, should I have to address the interruption?

Part one should be relativity straightforward in a time-optimized life. Part two is more fluid. Here you want to prepare yourself for what you will do if you are interrupted during that critical focus time.

- Am I ready to ask, "Sorry, can this please wait until later?"
- Do I have alternative times planned on my calendar to reschedule?
- Do I have questions ready to determine the seriousness of the intrusion?
- Am I ready to push back?
- Can I explain the challenges of what will happen if I do not get done with my work?

As the interruption happens, the questions start off by pushing the accountability back to the other person. The negative kicks in and comes back to you, to see if you are ready to push back if deflection does not work. Finally, you now seek to educate them on your priorities to see if they will and can adjust theirs.

The attention and assumption of interruption preparation is that a *person* and not a *thing* is breaking into your routine. I realize there will be non-human interruptions (like a car breaking down). That should be addressed in the last of the part-one questions.

INTERRUPTION: EXECUTION

You have planned part one and part two. You are excited to have some good, productive, and focused quality time ready. Things are going great and then *it* happens. It is totally natural for those negative emotions to kick in. Timothy Ferris in his book, *The 4-Hour Workweek,* puts this situation into a good perspective.

> *Blaming idiots for interruptions is like blaming clowns for scaring children—they can't help it. It's their nature. Then again, I had (who am I kidding—and have), on occasion, been known to create interruptions out of thin air. If you're anything like me, that makes us both occasional idiots.*[5]

I love the context of this quote. I have said before, I gave you permission to negatively manage external focus issues, with the caveat that you do it nicely. Timothy reminds us of that directly.

Now the interruption has occurred. Time-optimized PEC does not mean you suspend what you are doing and dive into the need of the interruption. You still are forced to stop, but your initiative is to get back to and focus on what you are doing. The questions are meant to be direct and quick but not rude.

- Sorry, can this please wait until later?
- Would it be possible to reschedule? Here are some alternatives . . .
- On a scale of 1 to 10, one being no issue and ten being a zombie apocalypse, how does your need rank? (Come up with your own qualifier if mine is too cheesy.)
- I appreciate your challenge, but I really need to get this done. I know it is important to you (their need to interrupt), but can we please do this at [the alternative times you propose]?
- Here is why this time (your need) is important to me. After hearing them, what alternatives can we do that help address my requirements?

I feel the need to talk about influence. Depending on your position within an organization or within your household, staving off interruptions may be in proportion to how much seniority or rank you can leverage. Always be mindful, be negative with *gentleness* and *respect* (particularly if you are the boss).

INTERRUPTION: CONTROL

"The impact of interruptions cannot be overstated. They kill our momentum. When we start again on our task, we can't simply pick up where we left off, we have to reorient ourselves, re-immerse, and re-gain our momentum."[6] Just as the *execution* phase is about speed, so is *control*. In reality, they are almost occurring simultaneously.

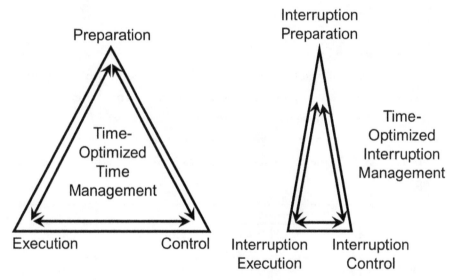

FIGURE 6:2 THE PEC OF INTERRUPTION MANAGEMENT

Let's quickly return to the part-one questions. Given that interruptions are happening in *the now*, it is hard to jump back to preparation when you get a question like, "Hey, do you have a second?" As a quick reminder, time optimization is a *continuous pursuit*, so time should be invested to evaluate or do a postmortem on occurrences to adjust your approach.

While there is always a preparation, execution, and control relationship in time optimization, Figure 6:2 demonstrates how E and C work much closer in tandem. This is the time when you negatively challenge yourself not to budge while pushing for swift and decisive closure to the interruption. Control means you may need to come back and rephrase the questions into statements.

- I am sorry—this needs to wait until later.
- Let's reschedule; here are some alternatives . . . please pick one that fits your schedule.
- On a scale of 1 to 10, one being no issue and ten being a zombie apocalypse, your need seems like a ___ to me.
- I appreciate your challenge, but I really need to get this done. I know it is important to you (their need to interrupt), but we need to pick an alternative time. Here are some options . . .
- Here is why this time (your need) is important to me, and I can't stop what I am doing right now.

As mentioned in Interruption: Execution, be mindful of your tone and delivery. If your boss is interrupting, you may need to address the need and then try to find time as quickly as possible to walk through preventative measures and solutions to when the disruptions need to occur. Should a subordinate come to you, watch that you don't deflate any enthusiasm or self-esteem. Finally, emotion can be very much in the mix when it comes to family. Be extra sensitive when trying to assert control.

Interruption Time Optimization				
Trait	*Preparation (Part 1)*	*Preparation (Part 2)*	*Execution*	*Control*
Wait until later	Time blocked off?	Ready to ask?	Ask definitively.	Declare definitively.
Alternative times	Different options for later?	Ready to propose?	Propose quickly.	Affirm quickly.
Level of need.	On to-do list?	Ask where on the scale?	Know their perspective.	Share you're a state of need.
Alternative times (again)	Different options for later?	Ready to propose again?	Ask definitively again.	Declare definitively again.
Challenge of not getting work done	Alternative tasks to adjust?	Ready to contest?	Contest their need.	Tell of your needs.

FIGURE 6:3 THE PEC OF REDUCING INTERRUPTIONS

Managing interruptions is not being on stage waiting for the perfect mic-drop moment. It is not a time to flaunt your time-management prowess to others by shoving your optimization into their face. On the other hand, don't roll over and easily give in. If a task is important to you, make it known and even important to others by investing in the right preparation. Once you are into it and an interruption happens, execution and control will come quickly.

DIVYA'S STYLE

When I interviewed Dr. Jaitly for the book, I asked her, "Why are you successful at limiting interruptions?"

Before answering, she stated, "Let me first define *success* because I feel the word can be very subjective. Success for me has always been about spending every second of my life meaningfully. If I am going to be doing something, I have to be 100 percent in it and focused."

Being a leader means a lot of meetings and choices that need to be made for the best use of her time. This approach cannot happen for her unless there is good time planning on the front end that answers three questions.

- How will I meet someone?
- What is the purpose of the meeting?
- Why am I meeting someone?

The *how* applies to the method, the *what* defines the details, and the *why* pertains to the person or persons involved.

This has assisted Divya overcome early struggles in her career where she pushed past the trait of being a "people pleaser" to converting and being more confident in what she needs to accomplish.

To help limit interruptions, her calendar is a powerful tool for rescheduling the disruption. Divya is confident in her schedule, planning to be ready to redirect or suspend when there is a demand on her time that can't be met at that point.

Being an adept public speaker, Dr. Divya also uses a *defer* and *deflect* technique to move past the interruption quickly. In addition, she combines that with a short meditative or power nap process that allows her to mind to stay focused and sharp for when the interruptions come.

SAYING NO

I have lost some big opportunities in my career. There are many reasons and explanations. As a salesperson, a lot can be tied to the process and the signs I failed to see as I tried to convince a client or prospect to accept my product or service. Each case was a little painful. However, on rare occasions, I was the one to say *no*.

I had a warm lead with a prospect, but it ended up not working out. I had multiple conversations, great dialog, and a good connection. However, in the end, I held firm on what I was going to offer for my services. I told myself "no" to any additional changes to the project price. As a result, the potential customer decided against using my services. While I missed out on the income and client, I felt it was an example of practicing the time management of no.

From *Psychology Today*, "Many of us are afraid of conflict. We don't like others to be angry with us or critical of us. We therefore avoid saying 'no' when we are afraid that it will put us into conflict with someone else, whether that someone is an intimate partner, a colleague or friend, or a supervisor or boss."[7]

Only 25 percent of respondents to the Time Management Analysis (TMA) tool expressed they are fully confident in their ability to say no. That means, for the majority of us, we adjust our schedules and work to accommodate a need of someone else before we really have had a chance to consider the impact to us.

There are two types of *no*: internal and external.

When struggling with time management, people can allow themselves to be sidetracked, losing a sense of focus. Instead of maintaining a schedule or plan, they permit change (or lack of) when they should be telling themselves no. We actually covered this in the last chapter under the topics of procrastination and distractions, two time management killers that require you to say no to yourself.

Our attention in this chapter is time-optimizing the external *no*. Probably the most obvious instances are those requests, demands, needs, invites, and appeals from others. Almost always unplanned, they can significantly impact your productivity and disrupt work rhythm and concentration.

You might be thinking there is not a lot of daylight between interruptions and saying no. The distinction between the two is one of heavy *preparation* and *control* in PEC. Saying no is a little more intense on the negative scale but still executed with gentleness and respect.

Stating no to someone proactively occurs on the front end, not when you are in the middle of a task. It may be the fifth time you have been asked by a different neighbor to sponsor her child's school fundraiser. Whether you are invited to lead a project in a meeting or a committee at church, time optimization suffers. Figure 6:4 highlights the change in PEC focus by saying no.

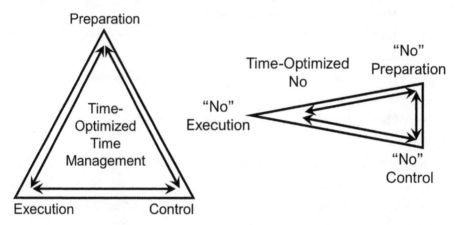

FIGURE 6:4 THE PEC OF *SAYING NO* MANAGEMENT

Best-selling author Stephen Covey puts it this way: "Keep in mind, you are always saying 'no' to something. If it isn't to the apparent, urgent things in your life, it is probably to the more fundamental, highly important things. Even when the urgent is good, the good can keep you from your best, keep you from your unique contribution, if you let it."[8] Stephen wants us to "organize and execute around balanced priorities."[9] That will require us to have embraced the other elements we have discussed in the book, as well as some of the ones to come. So let's show you more detail, the PEC way.

SAYING NO: PREPARATION

You have probably found the times you need to say no are usually when it is least expected. It can come in as, "Hey, you did a great job on that presentation. We would really like you to take the lead at the next three meetings and present as well."

Preparing yourself to say no is tied heavily back to time-optimized planning in Chapter 3. The more your time is developed and fits to your needs, the greater your confidence to hold firm and not add additional work to your schedule (unless you want to). Like we have been doing the last couple of chapters, it is time to add prompt questions to prime you to say no when appropriate.

- Have I set my short, long, and annual goals?
- Have I mapped out what my day, week, and next two weeks look like?
- Do I have any other assignments that need to get done that would impact taking on more?
- What would it mean to me to say yes to something new?

Knowing how to answer these questions at any time grooms the "no" to come out easier, not because you want to be negative, but because it helps you stay on a time-optimized path. While I have used "no" a lot, preparing this way also lets you give a solid "yes" that will benefit you and the one who asks.

SAYING NO: EXECUTION

Going back to Figure 6:4, the execution of no stands off to the side. It is more of an affirmation and answer to the questions asked in the preparation area. If you have prepared well, you should be able to move to control quickly.

- Do my short, long, and annual goals allow me to say yes?
- Does my mapped-out day, week, and next two weeks have openings for me to say yes?
- Do my other assignments that need to get done allow me to take on more and say yes?
- Knowing what it would mean, am I willing to make the necessary changes to say yes?

The intention is switched. Instead of jumping on the no, you discover if your time allows you to provide an affirmative answer. Execution literally is an internal calculation to control your answer.

This affords you the opportunity not to "beat around the bush or offer weak excuses or hem and haw. This only provides an opening for the other person. Don't delay or stall either. Provide a brief explanation if you feel you need to; however, don't feel compelled. The less said the better."[10]

SAYING NO: CONTROL

Because you have planned well, you whisk by execution, confidently answering all the questions. Now you need to deliver the news. Your control here is simply stated with "yes" or "no." Whether you choose to say one or the other, your choice is the result of you proactively knowing what is in your best interest. I realize there could be other responses like "maybe" or "tell me more" or "I'll think about it." They can be legitimate answers, but in a time-optimized approach, you will need to bring in PEC again in some form. That could be tied to planning (to know how to execute what you said yes to) and task administration (adding in all the activities tied to the new thing).

Now you are ready to deliver your no. Remember, do so with gentleness and respect. Jennifer Herrity with *Indeed* has some great examples to consider.[11]

- "Unfortunately, I have too much to do today. I can help you another time."
- "I'm flattered by your offer, but no thank you."
- "I know this isn't the answer you wanted, but I cannot accept your offer."
- "Thanks, but I'm all good. I appreciate the offer."
- "How thoughtful of you. I appreciate your offer, but this time, I'm simply too busy with work."
- "I know that's challenging for you, but I don't have the capacity to help you at the moment."

To assert the *control* of PEC means you are looking for a quick exit. Your no must be confident. Remember, this is your time.

Saying No: Time Optimization			
Trait	*Preparation*	*Execution*	*Control*
Goals	Short, long, annual set?	Can I say yes?	No?
Schedule mapped out	Opening to say yes?	Can I say yes?	No?
Other assignments	Opening to say yes?	Can I say yes?	No?
Something new	Makes changes to say yes?	Can I say yes?	No?

FIGURE 6:5 THE PEC OF CONTROLLING *NO*

As you leave this section, I want to recognize that saying no is hard. It can be difficult with a boss, family member, or friend. It is nice to feel needed and that others want to rely on you. The time-optimized way of saying no is all about getting out as quickly as possible. If that is difficult, dialog alternatives and seek greater clarity on the want or requirement. The time you invest here is not to say yes to assist the other party in giving them a pathway to get to their resolution without you in the mix.

DIVYA'S NO PHILOSOPHY

My discussion with Dr. Divya on this topic was enlightening to me. I do not think about having to choose my words carefully because I am a man; I am more concerned about how those words are delivered to my audience. She must approach the concept of saying no differently because of culture and being a woman.

"While assertive women, or women saying no, are not really accepted very well, I learned in my life and built a skill where you say no by using positive words. The egos of employers, leaders, partners, and clients get hurt if you say no outright," Divya explained.

As we referenced some examples previously, Dr. Jaitly has some suggestions too.

- How about we reconvene at a different time?
- Would you please give me two other alternatives?
- What other choices can we make?

Notice how the word *no* is not found at all. She emphasized, "Our brains' psychological and cognitive bearings do not respond well to 'no'. Even with our children. I have helped parents revamp their communication in this way. The older the children, the more you pivot the communication strategy (to positive words that convey 'no'), it changes the equation."

What I enjoyed about our conversation was Divya's ability to broaden our discussion to incorporate other elements of life. Because she was so focused on yes early in her life and business career, boundaries suffered. She did not sleep and eat well as her focus turned toward doing *more* and not necessarily doing what was *right*. Therefore, the ability or maybe even the need to say no is linked to personal care (which we will discuss in a couple of chapters). Dr. Divya firmly believes had she not learned to say no, she would be dealing with physical, mental, and emotional challenges today as a result.

The delivery of no is a delicate issue, so as you learn to execute it with the information in this chapter, consider the wider elements that Dr. Divya mentioned here to understand the impact on you in a broader way.

OUTSIDE IN

I said Chapter 5 was all about you. I started this one by saying, "This chapter is all about everyone else and the peripheral or outer happenings that cause us to lose focus." While I still hold on to that statement, Chapter 6 was also all about you.

Talking too much as a time-optimized approach is seeking to preemptively engage with those who might impact your ability to do your work. It is about "them," but the focus is to help you. Understand those who like to pontificate and seek them out first with the Talk Check-in, where you define the rules of engagement.

There is a technique in American football used by the ball carrier to keep a defender off of them. It is called the "stiff arm." Use that method (figuratively, please) to keep interruptions from impacting your productivity. PEC is your time-optimization strategy; it is your non-contact stiff arm.

Saying no stinks. As the author of this book, I still struggle to utter that word. Having said that, when you plan for "the ask" that you don't expect, you have created those internal reasons to justify the external no. There may be times when your declines cause issues and awkwardness. However, unless it is a life-threatening situation, in many instances, the person asking for your assistance is not relying on you only.

The internal *and* external focus are so important to your time optimization. We will return to them in Chapter 10. We move to the organization of time optimization next, where again, you find it is all about you.

CHAPTER 7

Time-Optimized Organization

Simply moving it [an event] around has a certain Zen [quality] to it and
allows me to chill when I make the change, and that makes it easy on my heart.
(Ellie Buck)

O
rganization can be a broad topic. For time-optimized organization, there
needs to be a cause and effect. We can be controlled/controlling but not
productive. Our work area might be in order but quiet because we are not
taking advantage of that organized area to act efficiently or time execute.

Growing up in the suburbs of Chicago, our next-door neighbor was a long-
time government employee who was an amateur pilot and loved to build things.
In the basement and garage of his house, he was constructing a replica World War
II Boeing-Stearman military trainer aircraft.

Because of his lengthy service, he decided to retire early and bought a specially
built house in Florida. He and his wife lived in a residential community with a

small airstrip where the garage was a mini-hanger for storing his soon-to-be-completed airplane. I remember the day they moved out. Our neighbors required two moving trucks, one for their personal goods and one for the unfinished airplane.

The next year, we visited them in their new home and check out the progress of the plane. The work he'd done was amazing. So was the quality of his craftsmanship. Also impressive was the workspace. Everything was clean and organized, not a spot of dirt anywhere. Tools were in order, spare parts set in a particular spot, and even the cleaning supplies were placed with all the labels facing out. He knew where everything was located.

The problem—if you want to call it that—became inaction. After finishing the biplane, our former neighbor paid a test pilot to fly it and certify the aircraft was functional. He got it approved for flight, but it never left his garage until it was sold years later. He had developed a fear of flying. The hanger sat quiet: neat, clean, and arranged. But no action or purpose was tied to that organization.

Time-optimized organization is about *action*, designed and structured action tied to—you guessed it—PEC.

A TIME-OPTIMIZED ORGANIZED PERSON—ELLIE BUCK

You have probably speculated by the last name that there is a personal connection with Ellie. She is my daughter-in-law. When I was working on the outline for this book and thought about including people I know to interview, she was probably the first to come to mind.

As a parent, this is where I am going to throw my oldest child under the bus. Before Ellie, Kenneth was, let's just say, *messy*. Going to visit where he lived required a strong immune system and the need to be up-to-date on all your shots. Enter Ellie, and she has enough organizational strength for the two of them.

Ellie is what is known as a "Cusper." Simply put, this is a person born on the cusp or border of two generations. She considers herself a millennial, and not Gen Z, because growing up in a rural area in the woods, there was no internet.

Having well-educated parents (five degrees between them), she naturally grew up in a structured environment. Ellie's biggest hobby was reading. A clear-cut sign of her organizational prowess came about during high school. "I was the kid who really liked getting those agendas they would make us all use. While everyone else hated them, I thought they were 'sweet.'" If there was no schedule available, she made her own through the bullet journal process. "It is an organizational tool that is aesthetically pleasing and allows creativity through organization," she explained.

When Ellie entered college, Google Calendar became her favorite app. It allows for ease of adjustments, and, as she emphasized, "It is like a living document that always changes."

Her organizational abilities helped her receive two degrees, an undergraduate Bachelor of Art in Art History and an MBA with a marketing focus.

When I asked Ellie how she approached her time management, she was direct. "I think I almost do it too well, which sounds insane. But I really can't function without the organization because I like it so much."

If you think she is boasting, she shared her screen with me and showed me her calendar. I was in time-optimized geek heaven. By being this detailed, Ellie knows how to access the information quickly and does not have to waste time trying to find it or figure out "where the grocery list went."

My son Kenneth did amazingly well marrying Ellie. Just that act alone raised his time optimization exponentially.

FINISHING WHAT YOU START

I have repeated myself a lot in this book (yay PEC), and I am going to do that again here. As noted back in Chapter 2, there is a difference between completing assignments and finishing what you started.

> *Completing assignments is tied to meeting an obligation to you or to others and is bound to a specific pursuit or endeavor. Finishing what you start is ongoing and mindset-driven. As activities are completed, there is less to juggle or rearrange. It is an attitude set well for PEC. You constantly prepare to always execute and control the outcome. That's proactive organization.*

The time approach to finishing is linear in nature. Your aspiration is to power forward, see progress, not sit, and if possible, not go backward or repeat. The time optimization of finishing is not living in the moment or evaluating the situation forever; it is you giving yourself a kick in the butt to get moving. Therefore, let's use the familiar PEC approach, which we have done in the last couple of chapters.

ORGANIZED FINISHING: PREPARATION

Let's clarify something about this form of provision. When you engage in the preparation of finishing, it is because you are having a problem with the PEC of an already established project or task. Somewhere in the execution and control, you are stuck or in limbo, unable to move forward; you have hit a wall (Figure 7:1)

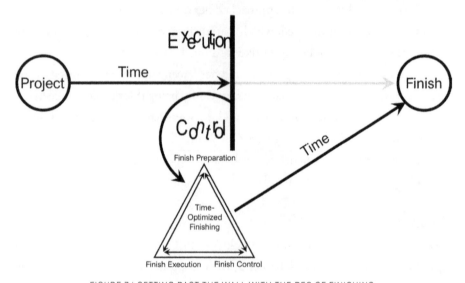

FIGURE 7:1 GETTING PAST THE WALL WITH THE PEC OF FINISHING

Your issue is not with the initial preparation. If that was the case, you could just apply the traditional PEC model and get back at it. It is different from procrastination, where internally you make excuses. The lack of finishing lies somewhere in the organization. Therefore, the preparation phase here represents a series of questions to be asked about the organizational nature of execution and control.

- Is my workspace organized to get at everything I need?
- What other tools or resources do I need to move forward?
- Do I know where to get access to any additional resources?
- Am I seeking organizational perfection to be able to produce?
- What other priorities need to shift for me to move forward?

These are inquiries you ask yourself to involve your tangible surroundings, internal perspective, and current workload. Each one (or all) might be keeping you from going around the wall of organizational delay that has been created.

ORGANIZED FINISHING: EXECUTION

There has been an affirmation of your task or project through the finishing preparation and you begin to execute again. Through this segment, the questions you can ask to uphold the queries addressed in finishing time-optimized preparation are here:

- Is my workspace helping or hurting progress?
- Are the other tools I added helping?
- Do I need to access additional resources?
- Am I moving forward even if everything is not perfect?
- Am I treating this as a high-priority item?

Your goal here is not to stop again. To highlight once more, organizational time optimization pushes cause to create an effect.

ORGANIZED FINISHING: CONTROL

Continuing the affirmation premise, finishing control is specific. You simply sustain the questions you asked as you executed.

- My workspace is helping the process.
- The other tools I added are helping.
- I have accessed any additional resources.
- I am moving forward even if everything is not perfect.
- This as a high-priority item.

"You've made the decision, made the plan and carried on to see the project through. It feels great to get a huge task off your plate, but there's one last important step to finishing: completion. When the task is done, make sure it's complete by ensuring it's stored, shared, or saved appropriately."[1] Wise advice from Adam Toren in his *Entrepreneur* online article.

Given that you have had to invest more time in the finishing time optimization process, it is important to get closure. The PEC of finishing will give you that.

Organized Finishing Time Optimization			
Trait	*Preparation*	*Execution*	*Control*
Workspace	Organized?	Helping?	Affirm execution
Tools	Add additional?	Helping?	Affirm execution
Resources	Able to access?	Have I accessed?	Affirm execution
Perfection	Can I move without it?	Am I moving without it?	Affirm execution
High priority	Am I treating it as one?	Am I moving forward?	Affirm execution

FIGURE 7:2 TIME-OPTIMIZED ORGANIZED FINISHING

ELLIE'S FINISH

Let's return to our millennial master organizer. As she was introduced at the beginning of the chapter, you learned Ellie controls her time well and finishing is important.

To ensure that happens, she starts with questions like, "Do I actually think I can accomplish this thing or project? If not, who do I need to talk to, to make sure I can get it done?" This self-evaluation sets the correct tone and expectation for herself.

Ellie also adds more time on top of what she originally plans in the preparation phase. That provides her with "wiggle room" to get around any roadblocks that might come up in completing a task or project.

Being a person of habit, Ellie will use her past experience to guide her as she executes a job. The past helps define the present project, to get it done on time in the future.

Ellie's career to date has been doing marketing for non-profit organizations. Typically, these are not in large-scale departments, and in her current role, she is a department of one. By virtue of her work, Ellie is beholden to a lot of other people, needing information from them before she can share that information with the world. This can be frustrating for her when others do not share her passion for organization and timeliness. When that happens, she jumps back into *preparation* mode and adjusts to add the right amount of additional time to *control* the finish.

By doing this, it allows Ellie, "to give myself a second chance if everyone else is not ready."

While Ellie is a great trouble-shooter, she realizes that will only get her so far. Therefore, she continues to seek additional education and more formal processes to help bring value to her time-management journey.

If something needs to be done, Ellie will see it to the finish.

THAT WAS QUICK

You might be thinking this section went by pretty quickly, and you are right. The PEC of finishing is targeted and tied to organization. Therefore, I have been direct and to the point. I am saving your reading time here to invest more in calendar time optimization because so much of overall PEC is done through the calendar.

USING A CALENDAR

I will get into the details in Chapter 10 on how you can integrate time optimization into your life, and calendaring will play a key role. I think a calendar is such a foundational tool. Hardly a day goes by where we do not look at one in some form (usually multiple times), yet it is so underutilized. David Allen notes in his book, *Getting Things Done*, the key role calendars play in productivity.

> *You need to trust your calendar as sacred territory, reflecting the exact hard edges of your day's commitments, which should be noticeable at a glance while you are on the run. That'll be much easier if the only things in there are those that you absolutely have to get done, or know about, on that day. When the calendar is regulated to its proper role in organizing, the majority of the actions you need to do are left in the category of "as soon as possible, against all the other things I have to do."*[2]

According to the data collected in the completed Time Management Analysis (TMA) assessments, over 20 percent of the respondents don't use a calendar. Only 27 percent said they operate their calendar to its fullest extent. As a time-management nerd, that is just crazy to me!

We are going to break our routine here and shift how the advice will be presented. Like with task management back in Chapter 4, we will journey through a general process to use for an electronic calendar. Again, I am not averse to the use of paper calendars and planners. I just find that in today's digital world of rapid change, you save time and effort when working from a screen rather than from paper.

My suggestion also remains that in-depth planning is best done using a computer with a nice-sized screen. Make use of the phone and tablet for adjustments and updates. I know—that might be old-school, leading some of you to say, "What a boomer."

As was stated back in "Maintaining a Task List," well over 90 percent of email systems you are using today (Google, Apple, Microsoft) have a calendar structure built into the service. So the examples I highlight are based on the "big three" because they share many of the same characteristics.

With the prerequisites out of the way, time-optimized calendaring hits at a variety of levels. *Calendar General Settings* are the foundational elements and set-up that guide you. *Productive Zone* adds a layer of intensity, helping you schedule work for when you are ready to get the most done. *Proactive Calendaring* is about your mindset and approach. Then we come back to PEC again with *Fill in the Blanks*, *Busy or Not*, and *Change or Not*.

GENERAL CALENDAR SETTINGS

Customization of your calendar can be an amazing way to bring time value and optimization to life. I am confident many of you reading this book have adjusted the look to benefit your scheduling and managing of time. However, so many of the clients I work with have never done a review of all the options afforded to them in just setting up their calendars. So, whether you are a novice or expert, we are going to walk our way through the settings that will provide you with a beneficial impact as you do your calendaring. We will quickly introduce a subject, give an explanation, and move onto the next. Here we go.

LIMIT YOURSELF

Too many people work from too many calendars. One for work, one for home, one for the kids, one for clubs or associations. For most of us, our work calendar has the most activity. If needed, seek permission from your employer to see if you can plan personal activities in one place. If that is not possible, then choose one other option and forward all events to one calendar. Your goal is not to have to look in multiple places. The good news is that you can share calendars between systems to see them in one spot.

SETTING THE WEEK

Ensure your calendar is on a full-week (Sun–Sat) view. This allows for the addition of personal events. My wife Susan sets her week to start on Monday. As a pastor, her heaviest workday can be on Sunday. By making that the last day of the week, she uses the preceding days as planning for Sunday. Remember, use whatever best matches your lifestyle.

Traditional Full-Week Set						
Sun	Mon	Tue	Wed	Thu	Fri	Sat

Monday Full-Week Set						
Mon	Tue	Wed	Thu	Fri	Sat	Sun

FIGURE 7:3 THE TWO PREFERRED CALENDAR WEEKLY CONFIGURATIONS

CREATING THE WORK ZONE

A work schedule is not always defined, and for many of you, it is flexible. Where applicable, set your works hours in place; that will adjust your calendar view (on a laptop or desktop) to those hours. It will make it much easier to plan your day.

HOLIDAYS

Import the holidays for your home country and, if you work internationally, the holidays of the countries you deal with on a regular basis. Whether you celebrate the holiday or not, having it visible as a reminder will help your time engagement with others.

ADDING TIME ZONES

Depending on your electronic calendar of choice, you can add one or more additional time zones to your view. This will allow you to better plan the best times to reach out or schedule meetings. I can tell you from firsthand experience, this has saved me a lot of time when dealing with my partner, clients, and friends in India.

IST	EST
	8 AM
6 PM	
	9 AM
7 PM	
	10 AM
8 PM	
	11 AM

FIGURE 7:4 ADDING AN EXTRA TIME ZONE TO YOUR CALENDAR

TIME SCALE

Every calendar I have seen sets the default at thirty-minute increments. This will work for most people. However, if you attend a lot of back-to-back meetings and generally have a full calendar because of that, consider changing the scale to fifteen minutes. This will make it easier for you to schedule forty-five-minute meetings and allow for buffer time between them.

APPOINTMENTS

My experience with calendars has appointments set for a thirty-minute duration. Unless a majority of your meetings run longer or shorter, there are negligible time savings to change the default.

BRINGING IN THE TASK VIEW

I use separate software for the setting and execution of my tasks (Microsoft To Do for me, but you can have Goggle Task or Apple Reminders). Still, I also change the view on my calendar to include the task or to-do bar. Having this visible and next to your schedule aids in correlating your calendar to your tasks for any given day. You'll be shown a visual dose of reality on your ability to honor any calendar obligations against the planned to-dos.

Setting your calendar should be a personal experience. Make it work for you and your needs. Invest the time to align the look and feel with what you want to accomplish.

I am sure many of you are thinking, "Why didn't he mention _____?" There are numerous tricks and options I could have explored, but this is about the PEC of time optimization. These settings open you to the main elements of calendar preparation, execution, and control.

PRODUCTIVE ZONE

I am a morning person. Just about every day, I am up at 5 a.m. (sometimes to the consternation of my wife). I find I am the most productive in the morning, and, like any combustible engine, the fuel in the tank moves from full to empty as the day goes along. (Susan is the same. She just wishes the engine was started a little later, say at sunrise.)

Much of what defines our most productive time can be tied to our circadian rhythms, or internal biological clocks.

> The timing of our internal clock changes as we age (remember staying up until 2 a.m. as a teenager?). So while the sweet spot for young adults is early afternoon, the prime productivity window shifts earlier as we get older. Our genetics and social environments can also impact our internal rhythm. If your friends are all night owls, for example, you might adjust to staying up late. Or if your job requires you to be up at the crack of dawn, you might find yourself becoming a morning person.[3]

Based on this, stop and review where personal and professional impact your twenty-four-hour cycle.

I used to have to work the overnight shift, coming in at 11:00 p.m. and working until 8:30 a.m. I never felt like I was a night person. However, I did know that I was the strongest at the beginning of my shift, fought through the 2 a.m. to 4 a.m. lull, and then saw a ramp up from 6 a.m. to the end of the shift (just because more people came in to work their traditional morning period).

Know your productive time, turn it into a zone of opportunity, and plan accordingly. Don't be selfish with this knowledge. Discuss with your boss, coworkers, friends, and even family. Use it to negotiate protected time, reach out to important clients, set important meetings, and work on high-value projects or tasks.

Prepare to be industrious, execute in that time, and control your outcome by guarding the duration when you are most efficient. Let it be visibly seen on your calendar.

PROACTIVE CALENDARING

Who runs your calendar, you or the calendar? I have asked this question many times of direct reports and clients. When I inquire about seeing a person's calendar, many times I find something like Figure 7:5.

FIGURE 7:5 REACTIVE CALENDAR PLANNING

It is the work calendar, normally filled with meetings they need to attend, whether created by themselves or someone else, populated with a lot of blank time. This leads to a typical type of conversation about being proactive versus reactive.

> **Me:** "Tell me about your current schedule. Why does your calendar look like this?"

> **Person:** "These are times when I am away from my desk and have to be somewhere else."

> **Me:** "What do you do in and during the blank time?"

> **Person:** "I work on my tasks and things I need to get done that day."

> **Me:** "What happens if a last-minute meeting pops up on your calendar?"

> **Person:** "I'll accept, go during that time, come back, and pick up where I left off."

I get it. This is a simplified conversation. There are a host of reasons why a calendar could look like this. You may not be able to easily say no to items that can come onto your schedule (but we do have a way to combat that back in the last chapter). The level of flexibility and availability varies significantly, depending on job and lifestyle. Nonetheless, let's come back to our time optimization definition. *It is a continuous pursuit of the right preparation, along with the right execution, to escalate broad control over personal productivity.* Even among a host of known and unknown disruptions, PEC can and should be employed.

FILL IN THE BLANKS: PREPARATION

Let's say your productivity zone is from 9 a.m. to 2 p.m. This is not to declare no work gets done outside that region or that your work quality diminishes (though that will happen if you work too many hours). This is the time when you know you can really crank out some productivity. I also don't recommend you become so rigid as to impact relationships.

Going back to our original example in Figure 7:5, let's hard block the existing activities and say they are formal, immovable time as shown in Figure 7:6.

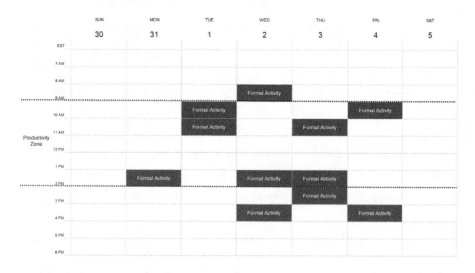

FIGURE 7:6 THE PRODUCTIVITY ZONE

Time-optimized calendar planning now fills the blanks with the most productive activities.

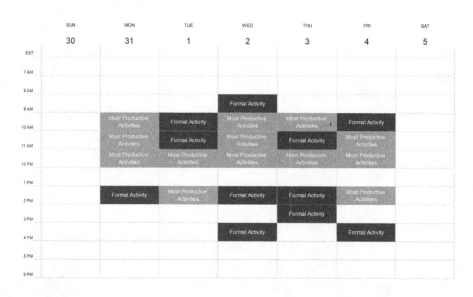

FIGURE 7:7 ACTIVITIES IN THE PRODUCTIVITY ZONE

Next, to no one's surprise, the other hours are filled with less productive activities. Consider placement here of lower-level tasks and things that would require less focus and attention (See Figure 7:8).

	SUN 30	MON 31	TUE 1	WED 2	THU 3	FRI 4	SAT 5
EST							
7 AM							
8 AM							
9 AM		Less Productive Activities	Less Productive Activities	Formal Activity	Less Productive Activities	Less Productive Activities	
10 AM		Most Productive Activities	Formal Activity	Most Productive Activities	Most Productive Activities	Formal Activity	
11 AM		Most Productive Activities	Formal Activity	Most Productive Activities	Formal Activity	Most Productive Activities	
12 PM		Most Productive Activities	Most Productive Activities	Most Productive Activities	Most Productive Activities	Most Productive Activities	
1 PM							
2 PM		Formal Activity	Most Productive Activities	Formal Activity	Formal Activity	Most Productive Activities	
3 PM		Less Productive Activities	Less Productive Activities	Less Productive Activities	Formal Activity	Less Productive Activities	
4 PM		Less Productive Activities	Less Productive Activities	Formal Activity	Less Productive Activities	Formal Activity	
5 PM		Less Productive Activities	Less Productive Activities	Less Productive Activities	Less Productive Activities	Less Productive Activities	
6 PM							

FIGURE 7:8 LESS PRODUCTIVE ACTIVITIES

Finally, as shown in Figure 7:9, last (but not necessarily least) include personal activities to fill in all the blanks.

	SUN 30	MON 31	TUE 1	WED 2	THU 3	FRI 4	SAT 5
EST							
7 AM							
8 AM	Personal Activities	Personal Activities	Personal Activities	Personal Activities	Personal Activities	Personal Activities	Personal Activities
9 AM	Personal Activities	Less Productive Activities	Less Productive Activities	Formal Activity	Less Productive Activities	Less Productive Activities	Personal Activities
10 AM	Personal Activities	Most Productive Activities	Formal Activity	Most Productive Activities	Most Productive Activities	Formal Activity	Personal Activities
11 AM	Personal Activities	Most Productive Activities	Formal Activity	Most Productive Activities	Formal Activity	Most Productive Activities	Personal Activities
12 PM	Personal Activities	Most Productive Activities	Most Productive Activities	Most Productive Activities	Most Productive Activities	Most Productive Activities	Personal Activities
1 PM	Personal Activities	Personal Activities	Personal Activities	Personal Activities	Personal Activities	Personal Activities	Personal Activities
2 PM	Personal Activities	Formal Activity	Most Productive Activities	Formal Activity	Formal Activity	Most Productive Activities	Personal Activities
3 PM	Personal Activities	Less Productive Activities	Less Productive Activities	Less Productive Activities	Formal Activity	Less Productive Activities	Personal Activities
4 PM	Personal Activities	Less Productive Activities	Less Productive Activities	Formal Activity	Less Productive Activities	Formal Activity	Personal Activities
5 PM	Personal Activities	Less Productive Activities	Less Productive Activities	Less Productive Activities	Less Productive Activities	Less Productive Activities	Personal Activities
6 PM	Personal Activities	Personal Activities	Personal Activities	Personal Activities	Personal Activities	Personal Activities	Personal Activities

FIGURE 7:9 THE FULLY PLANNED CALENDAR

Albeit a simplistic explanation, *fill in the blanks* is a solid outline to provide for every hour of your calendar with planned meeting times and activities. It honors the continuous nature of time optimization and gets the optics from a reactive open calendar to a full and proactive schedule, giving you the opportunity to better prioritize what is important to you.

Having a full calendar draws in many other categories we have discussed. Procrastination, motivation, distractions, interruptions, and saying no can be better prevented and obscured by filling in the blanks.

Now that the upcoming week is planned, do it for the next week. Yes, that is right; plan out for two weeks! No, I am not typing this with some over-the-top horror film laugh. Invest the time to go out for an extra week.

Fourteen days of planning brings in many other time-optimized attributes. You enhance internal focus, resisting the urge to procrastinate and get distracted. You inoculate yourself from the pain of external interruptions and prepare for providing the respectful and gentle "no."

About this time, a number of readers are wondering if this is even possible. Right now, when the days are fully planned, anyone else looking at the schedule will not see any openings. Should you participate in a lot of meetings or others rely on you for their time, this system may seem impractical. That is why it is time to move to the execution part using a calendar, where we choose to show ourselves busy or not.

BUSY OR NOT: EXECUTION

Planning every hour on your calendar does not mean you get to block out the world and sit comfortably in your isolation chamber in a blaze of productivity brilliance. As good as that sounds, the world has other plans.

Once every hour is planned, the time-optimized calendar execution method is to publicly declare your availability. I don't mean that you walk around work reading your schedule like a town crier. Each of the major calendar systems allows you to show a meeting/event as "Busy" or "Free." Depending on your brand, you may have other choices like "Working Elsewhere" or "Out of Office." You can introduce those if you would like, but for this execution purpose, we only need the first two.

Your main goal is to designate which events will show to others that the time is blocked or open. By setting an event on your calendar as *free* means you see it, but it shows blank or invisible to anyone else who can see your calendar or a client who wants to book an appointment through any system that might be in place.

Should you choose to block the time as busy (and it is not a meeting), remember to inform those who might be affected and gain permission from a supervisor if needed. This procedure will not prevent the "meeting bully" from throwing that late-breaking, do or die, must-have, stop everything summit. The process will give you ammunition to push back (with gentleness and respect) by showing you had already planned that time for other purposes.

Simply put, you execute calendar usage by declaring you are open to the possibility of being at someone else's disposal.

CHANGE OR NOT: CONTROL

Every hour is planned, and you show busy or not. That does not and will not stop change. You or others will adjust meetings. Emergencies will happen. Things will get canceled.

Control, in this case, is narrow and specific. Change or not? *Do I need to adjust my schedule going forward to account for this change?*

If the adjustment or addition occurs in a less productive activity timeframe, you may just choose to deal with the interruption and not adjust anything else. Should you prefer to make a change or adjustment, calendar time optimization sends you back to *preparation* to make the necessary adjustments to account for less time.

As a reminder, you are managing your to-dos independently of the calendar. Yes, I encourage the task list to be up next to your schedule, but task management will be tied more to re-prioritization and not necessarily change—like the calendar.

The PEC of using a calendar is heavy on the *P* and narrow on the *E* and the *C*. All can contain a level of intensity and challenge, but as Figure 7:10 shows, the process leans heavily into preparation.

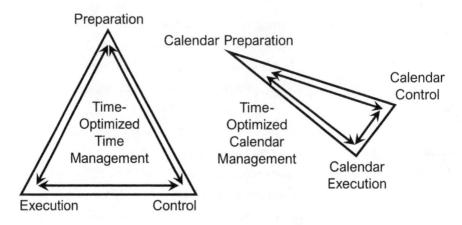

FIGURE 7:10 THE PEC OF CALENDAR MANAGEMENT

TIME BLOCKING

A quick word about the concept of Time Blocking. "Time blocking is the practice of planning your schedule for the day in advance by blocking every hour of your day for specific tasks and responsibilities."[4]

I have subtly talked about and around this by recommending your task list be up and in view as you PEC your calendar. Time blocking links the two together, allocating specific times on your calendar to complete the tasks you have listed.

Time-blocking purists will allocate time on their calendars and then work that time until it is up. If they do not have their tasks complete, then the to-dos are reprioritized for another day where a time block has been created for the tasks. It can be an effective system and fits well into our time-optimized discussion. To be successful, you must have a solid understanding and execution of both your calendar and your tasks.

On occasion, a mentor of mine would council me to "creep, crawl, walk, run." If this section inspires you to be disciplined on calendar time optimization, don't introduce time blocking until you are comfortable at least "walking" with your calendar and tasks.

ELLIE'S CALENDAR—COLOR-CODING

While some readers might be wondering, "He covered time blocking, where is color-coding or blocking?" I saved it for here because Ellie lives by it. In fact, we both got excited and shared the color process we each use when I interviewed her for this book.

Calendar systems allow you to set a general color scheme. If you like green, your calendar will have various shades of green as you work your schedule. Color-coding is when you choose to categorize meetings with a particular hue, creating a visually impactful view, allowing you to readily identify the type of activity, event, or meeting taking up a set timeframe.

I color-code based on the categories of my business. For example, If I am going to have a meeting with a client on leadership, that will show in yellow. When it is related to time management, I set it purple. Ellie has a different approach; she sets her colors by mood or theme. Because her calendar is fluid, she might have more than one event in each time allocation. Setting different colors to her "mood" helps prioritize that which stands out as most important.

Calendar programs also allow for a lot of information to be populated besides the title. Here, Ellie blends tasks and calendaring more than most. She will put her entire grocery list in that calendar event, so when she goes shopping, it is right there on her phone.

To affirm my view, I asked Ellie where she spent most of her time using her calendar. "Oh, it is almost exclusively on desktop. Anything else is just too clunky. I really only refer to my calendar on my phone."

I feel so encouraged that my book feels intergenerational now. As soon as my son Kenneth reads this, there will be a "Go ahead and think that . . . boomer."

I slipped in earlier that it is a good habit to plan your calendar with every hour filled at least two weeks out. In the case of Ellie, she also works out a year in advance. Let her clarify: "I do it for big stuff, like vacations or holiday travel. It does not necessarily need to be written in stone; it can be aspirational as well."

Change will happen, so I asked Ellie how she manages that change with such a full calendar. "That is why I went to an electronic calendar format and away from a paper calendar or planner because I move things around so easily. It helps when I get too attached to an event. Simply moving it around has a certain Zen [quality] to it and allows me to chill when I make the change, and that makes it easy on my heart."

I might be the only person excited about this discussion (well, maybe Ellie as well). Whether you color-code or not, start down Ellie's path, and it will turn into a wide road of time optimization.

BEING ORGANIZED

The concept of being organized and general organization can be broad. Let me start at the outset by saying I am not expecting anyone to become a version of the hyper-organized Sheldon Cooper,[5] from the television series *Big Bang Theory*, or an earlier television character, Adrian Monk,[6] from the self-titled show called *Monk*. I am also not going through a set-by-step process to reduce and remove clutter. As I mentioned previously, this is about action.

Being organized in a time-optimized framework highlights the ways in which you put structure into your life and, at the very least, does not cause you to delay or waste time. All the way back in Chapter 2, I mentioned the condition of my wife's office and how it appears to be jumbled and disorderly. However, she knows where to find the items she needs (I think it is a superpower). On the surface, does she appear organized? No. Can she get to the things she needs quickly? Yes.

Therefore, if I may be so bold, you will find the right level of organization by following all the various aspects of PEC covered in this book. The other priority categories become the lug nuts for organization. "Wheel Lug Nuts are a tapered nut used to fasten the wheel to the threaded wheel studs connected to your car's axle. Wheel Lug Bolts fasten the wheel of your car to the wheel's hub or brake drum."[7]

Dedicated *planning* helps shape the unknown. Establishing *personal goals* and *mapping ahead* can configure your view of the future. Using *meetings* as a place of productivity minimizes subsequent blocks of wasted time. The dedication of *completing assignments* lets you concentrate on new work more efficiently.

Embracing the benefits of *task design* arranges your to-dos better. A properly worked *task list* formats your workload correctly. *Prioritizing* the list in the best way lays out patterns of order. Giving up *multitasking* lets you associate the right task energy to the right time.

Strengthening your *internal focus* opens your mind to internal organization. Stop *procrastinating* and you will relieve the activity pressure. Stay *positively motivated* and you have the energy to tackle items that may be stacking up. Eliminate *distractions* and you stay on task and message.

Pinpoint those areas of *external focus* that constitute poor time usage. *Too much talk* is not progress; it can lead to organizational frustration (not just for you, but for others). Extinguish *interruptions* that keep you from patterns of time regulation. Learn the power of saying no in relation to order.

While this will be covered in detail in the next chapter, *personal care* gives you organizational energy. *Sleeping* changes your mind and body. *Taking breaks* resets your thinking and can organize your thoughts. *Exercise* is positive stress giving you energy reserve to manage the events of life. *Spirituality* organizes your thoughts and actions outside of yourself. How you choose to practice can bring about order.

Whether you need to put them on or tighten them up, your time-optimized priority lug nuts are keeping the organizational tire attached to the car. Take them away, and the wheel falls off. That would be a mess for your time optimization.

FIGURE 7:11 THE LUG NUTS OF TIME-OPTIMIZED ORGANIZATION

ELLIE'S VIEW

Ellie's overall view of organization is, "Everything is in its own spot. It is more than just time but also your space. I like to have a nice clean workspace so that I feel comfortable in it. For me, organization is associated with comfort for both professional and personal; it allows me to relax."

Her general routine to maintain that comfort starts with maintaining her calendar. Ellie also invests the time to give her desk a thorough cleaning once a week to help reset the space but also her mindset. "It makes me feel more professional on the outside and then more functional on the inside."

At home, she has had to learn to compromise—establish boundaries but know the standards she has set may not apply to her husband. I think that is a great approach, particularly if you (the reader) adopt and see success in time-optimization methods from this book. There are no factors in play that necessitate any change in behavior for others in your household (unless you give them this book). Therefore, whether personal or professional, be ready to negotiate, or even look the other way, as you refine your productivity.

As we wrapped up our conversation, Ellie emphasized, "Sometimes to get organized, I need to jump start myself to organize that one space or activity, which is often the hardest part. Once [I] have a system in place, I can keep that up forever."

This aligns with her overall philosophy whereby you choose one thing and focus on that until you have reached the level of organization you need, then start on the next. It is an organization of action—and of PEC.

CHAPTER 8

Time-Optimized Personal Care

Being in the military you learn, even though I did not want to get up, I was pushing myself much further than I would have, normally. You then realize you just feel great the rest of the day. When it is done, you still feel amazing.
(Julie Blacutt)

W ay back at the beginning of the book, I noted a variety of personal qualifiers on my expertise. Just to remind you, I am not in the medical field. I try to exercise regularly but I am no personal trainer. I have some semblance of a good diet because I have a wife who pays attention to that. I am also not a pastor, swami, shaman, or religious guru.

However, I am a firm believer (based on evidence from those specialized) that the way we approach our physical, mental, and spiritual selves can be beneficial or detrimental to time optimization. I work a PEC program of personal care, and it is a continuous process.

Personal care is a broad and wide topic. There are numerous industries tied to the subject. The four items I chose for this book are included because I saw a correlation between them and time optimization. In the PEC method, sleep and breaks are defined and can be time-optimized without having to establish elaborate plans and strategies. Exercise introduces more complexity, depending on what you want to do, but it has a lot of structure, and it is easy to measure. The hardest to quantify and qualify is spirituality, particularly because it means so many things to so many people.

Some of you may have remembered; I said this would be a short chapter, and that still kind of holds true. You will see a lot of references here from people who know more than me as a way to help support my position. In fact, let's move onto Julie, the featured time-optimized person for this chapter.

A TIME-OPTIMIZED PERSONAL-CARE PERSON—JULIE BLACUTT

I got to know Julie Blacutt in an interesting way. I left a really great job to start my company, Kairos Management Solutions. I led the sales efforts for multiple brands and companies for a parent corporation. Each day brought something different. However, I felt the call to entrepreneurship and left my previous employer. As they searched for the next vice president of Business Development, they asked if I could stay on in a consulting role to help with the transition. I even participated in the hiring process.

My replacement was Julie. I stayed on another six weeks and helped during the transition and felt she was a great fit for the organization. In the course of our conversations, I asked her to take the Time Management Analysis and found she scored really well across the board but felt she would be a great addition to our personal care discussion.

Julie grew up in Southern California, which, if you know anything about the United States, has a culture around fitness and health. Having a father as an engineer and a mother as a teacher meant they had a structured and consistent routine. After the events of September 11, 2001, she joined the military for a few years and after getting out, pursued a career in sales.

As a working mother, Julie juggles the demands of her job with two active children and all the events that come with that. While she feels somewhat in flux, there is a solid structure in place because there needs to be. By taking care of herself, she is able to manage her time well, ensuring she places quality time in her personal *and* professional life.

SLEEPING

Why do we sleep? There are many theories around that question. "[D]espite decades of research and many discoveries about other aspects of sleep, the question of why we sleep has been difficult to answer."[1] I don't know about you, but if I try to not sleep, I can't. So if there is no definitive conclusion to the *why* question, let's all own that it is necessary. It is a good investment of our time.

What is the right amount of sleep? Here, we might not all agree. Depending on your age, it varies. The way you live your life impacts how much time you want to devote to sleep. The Centers for Disease Control (CDC) for the United States government puts out their recommendations by age group.[2]

Age Group	Age	Recommended Hours of Sleep
Infant	4–12 months	12–16 hours per 24 hours (including naps)
Toddler	1–2 years	11–14 hours per 24 hours (including naps)
Pre-School	3–5 years	10–13 hours per 24 hours (including naps)
School Age	6–12 years	9–12 hours per 24 hours
Teen	13–18 years	8–10 hours per 24 hours
Adult	18–60 years	7 or more hours per night
	61–64 years	7–9 hours per night
	65+ years	7–8 hours per night

FIGURE 8:1 SLEEP CHART FROM THE CDC[2]

After reviewing multiple sources from places like John Hopkins Medicine[3], Medical News Today[4], and National Sleep Foundation[5], the suggested sleep amounts for adults range between seven and nine hours. For the application of PEC, we'll land in the middle at eight hours. Basically, you are time optimizing for twenty-four hours, two-thirds while you are awake and another one-third asleep.

"While sleeping, the body performs a number of repairing and maintaining processes that affect nearly every part of the body. As a result, a good night's sleep, or a lack of sleep, can impact the body both mentally and physically."[6]

Lest you think you can go for long periods with small amounts of sleep, watch out. "When we are sleep deprived, our focus, attention, and vigilance drift, making it more difficult to receive information. Without adequate sleep and rest, over-worked neurons can no longer function to coordinate information properly, and we lose our ability to access previously learned information."[7]

To put it in a more practical sense, a time-management leader in India, Brigadier Sushil Bhasin, has been sleep-deprived many times in his military career. However, in his book, *Million Dollar Second*, he presents a unique philosophy, born from years of experience.

> *Sleep becomes the first target in most time-management exercises. "Do all you can in a day and leave sleep for the balance of time," is one way many people treat sleep. Sleep has a great role in health and productivity and cannot be neglected. I have slept for 4 to 5 hours a night, many years of my life. It has worked well. I believed that by reducing my sleep I am creating more productive time. I now feel, one must resort to this with a deliberate, balanced approach. Depriving your body and mind of the rightful rest they deserve may not really be a "productive idea."*[8]

I am holding firm on the eight-hour suggestion. If you are not there now (by the way, neither am I. I am around seven), then let's cover the PEC of it.

SLEEP: PREPARATION

Remember, I am not a doctor, so preparation here is not methods or medication suggestions to help you get to sleep. My prescriptions of choice are the calendar and the alarm.

As we talked in the last chapter, the calendar is one of the most important tools for time optimization. Use it here as well and plan your sleep time into your schedule. Block it off and treat slumber as an event. Give yourself a buffer time between your last "awake" activity and when sleep begins to give your mind and body down time.

In addition, create or designate an alarm device (phone, watch, Alexa, etc.) for when you wake up but also for when to go to bed.

Sleep is one of the longest, if not the longest, events of the day. Account for it by putting it on your calendar.

SLEEP: EXECUTION

I have been trying to come up with some amazing anecdote or pithy saying for sleep execution, but the easiest way to express it here is to borrow Nike's slogan and say, "Just do it." Treat sleep like you are attending an important meeting. Be on time, be a full participant, and be good at it.

Execute well by removing any internally based distractions and externally based interruptions.

SLEEP: CONTROL

Sleep control is intentional. Your reward for doing it will be more energy and a healthier life. As Brigadier Bhasin mentioned before, do not relate sleep as a reactive activity, only to treat it as a "remainder" time after everything else is done.

WHAT ABOUT NAPS?

It has become more acceptable in certain industries to allow for naps in the workplace. Dr. Divya Jaitly (who was featured back in Chapter 6) is a proponent of short power naps, even if they are blocks of meditation or quieting the mind. These moments of rest help provide a focus for her.

Napping offers various benefits for healthy adults, including:

- Relaxation
- Reduced fatigue
- Increased alertness
- Improved mood
- Improved performance, including quicker reaction time and better memory[8]

For me to nap, I need to be in a specific place (like on my living room couch). "Napping isn't for everyone. Some people simply can't sleep during the day or have trouble sleeping in places other than their own beds, which napping sometimes requires."[9]

From a time-optimized standpoint, nap at your own pace. PEC would tell you to plan for it and integrate it into your schedule. However, I understand the ad hoc nature of napping, so just be mindful of what it can do to the rest of the day and what impact (positive or negative) it will have on what needs to be accomplished.

JULIE'S SLEEP

When we started our conversation about personal care, Julie confidently stated, "Sleep is something I never really had a problem with my whole life. I always have been good at it."

To help keep that in place, she enforces that with a solid exercise program. "If I am still having trouble getting to sleep, then no alcohol, and even a reduction in caffeine." Should there still be an issue, she will put on background noise or a sleep meditation to help quiet the brain.

Julie does not eat too late. "I think it is good to eat as early as possible—within reason—and if you can take a walk, even if it is ten to fifteen minutes, [do it]."

Her nightly routine is to get to bed by 10 p.m. and be up by 6 a.m.

Sleep is very important for her because, "With all that is going on, I appreciate all the things I have to do, and I want to show up in my best form."

Whether you are a natural sleeper like Julie or one who struggles with it, like me, these plans Julie uses can help anyone.

BREAKS

In the early phase of my career, I worked as an account manager, selling greeting cards and gift products. One of the major clients, a national drugstore chain, frequently opened new stores. If that happened in my territory, I was assigned the account by my employer.

As the sales rep, I was responsible for ensuring the department was set up correctly and ready for its grand opening. These departments were large, many well over one hundred linear feet in length. Setting up the initial fixtures (provided by my employer to the client) was time-consuming and challenging. Because of that, the drugstore sometimes provided workers to "assist," in the theory they would be installed correctly.

However, frequently, the "help" was more like a hindrance. Many did not have any experience building and installing a greeting card department. That was not the biggest challenge. Three times a day, they took "mandatory" breaks. The foreman would yell, "Break time!" Literally, whatever was being done totally stopped in that instant. You may have heard, "Drop what you are doing" before. In these cases, it was precisely that; I have watched framework being let go and slamming to the floor.

That experience somewhat jaded me in the idea of a work break. I felt these breaks interrupted and impeded productivity. So, for a long time, I never felt there was any worth or benefit. Chalk up another mistake on my part.

Now, breaks can be defined in many ways—from a vacation or holiday or a meal to a five-minute "coffee run." The question we ask on the Time Management Analysis (TMA) is the following:

I take at least one break during the day, not including lunch. (You intentionally leave your workspace and do another non-work related activity.)

Therefore, the guideline here is a meal plus something else. Not that "breaking bread" does not have time-optimized benefits; it means you need to at least add one more break on top of that during the day.

It may sound counterintuitive to say that stopping what you are doing benefits your productivity. However, there is an abundance of evidence and scientific studies that support this *good* interruption. "These breaks are essential in helping employees de-stress and re-charge for the rest of the workday. Regular breaks can also help improve overall job satisfaction."[10]

"Breaks can replenish the psychological costs associated with working hard, improve work performance, and boost energy."[11]

Highlighted in the book *Deep Work* is, "Instead of scheduling the occasional break from *distraction* so you can focus, you should instead schedule the occasional break *from focus* to give into distraction."[12]

Embrace the concept of getting away where you experience a physical and mental break. Let's see how it applies to PEC.

BREAK: PREPARATION

Maybe because I have a residual hangover from my greeting card fixture story, I do not propose a rigid or hard system. If you feel the need to formally place a break on the calendar to help you take it, then please, have at it. The challenge can be when you are focused. It may be best to benefit from the heightened productivity and stay at it versus dropping what you are doing because the calendar said so. Try giving yourself break zones so you can allow flexibility based on your workload (Figure 8.2).

FIGURE 8:2 CREATING BREAK ZONES

Staying with the fluid nature of breaks, I am also not going to give a definitive time. That must be defined by the type of work you do or the life you live. A common theme tends to run between fifteen and twenty minutes. "If taking a break is so important, then the length of that break is important, too. You want to make sure that your brain has time to do everything it needs to in order to make the break profitable."[13]

BREAK: EXECUTION

Let's start with that time-optimized break execution is *not*.

- Staying in the same place
- Jumping on social media
- Playing video games
- Eating
- Emailing and texting

Going back to Cal Newport's book, he brings up a concept called *productive meditation.*

> *The goal of productive meditation is to take a period in which you're occupied physically but not mentally—walking, jogging, driving, showering—and focus your attention on a single well-defined professional problem. Depending on your profession, this problem might be outlining an article, writing a talk, making progress on a proof, or attempting to sharpen a strategy. As in mindfulness meditation, you must continue to bring your attention back to the problem at hand when it wanders and stalls.*[14]

While this applies to longer periods, it also has great application to your break execution. Getting up and going for a walk or paying attention to something different from what you were doing will give the brain something else to focus on (professional or personal). You come back to the job with a renewed sense of creativity to finish what is up or set the stage for the next activity. Make the *break* productive for your brain.

BREAK: CONTROL

Break *control* can be elusive. Your workplace culture may even frown on it. As with all the other time-optimized solutions discussed in this book, you must be disciplined and see the benefits to you by investing this time. Therefore, if taking breaks is new to your routine, start small. Compare and reflect on your productivity at the times when you took a break compared to the times you did not. Are you able to see the real benefits of the miniature time off?

WHAT ABOUT DAYS OFF AND VACATIONS?

Let's briefly touch on vacations and days off. They fall outside the PEC of time-optimized breaks. However, they provide a much larger duration of the benefits highlighted in this section. A really well-researched resource to understand this is *The Hard Break* by Aaron Edelheit.

> There is an area of the brain that neurologists call the *default mode network*, which use[s] downtime from activity to try and make sense of what the brain has recently learned. This part of the brain considers problems, patterns, and memories—all while we think we are not doing anything. Creative people in particular have a more active *default mode network* than others.[15]

Whether it is a short period or a two-week vacation, let your *default mode network* be active because you are intentional in giving yourself a break.

JULIE'S BREAKS

Coming back to our personal-care person, Julie has an evolved natural process when it comes to her routine with breaks. She explained, "Usually around 10 a.m., I am ready for a cup of coffee and some kind of protein snack. That is how I take a formal break; my body helps me regulate it. It has been a pretty consistent rhythm for me."

Location plays a role in what else will happen during her break time. "If I am at home, I might take the dogs out and around the block. If I am in the office, I may take the opportunity to talk with other associates around the building."

Without positively interrupting herself, Julie feels sitting in one place takes a toll on her body. For long-term health, she makes it a point to get up and move around.

I asked her what she might recommend for people who struggle with taking breaks. She answered, "I am a little surprised so many people do not [take breaks]. With that said, I think people really need to decide what that break is going to be. Maybe it is once an hour that you take a five-minute break and set your watch or phone. Everybody needs to get out of their chair; it is not good for your hips, eyes, neck, or shoulders [to sit for long periods]."

Like so much we have discussed in the book, take Julie's advice and start small, then work your way into a solid routine—not only for time optimization but for your health.

EXERCISE

Of those who have taken the Time Management Analysis (TMA), only four in ten agree or strongly agree with the scenario, *"I exercise regularly. (You engage in exercise at least 3 times a week for at least 30 minutes each session)."*

The data compiled by the Centers for Disease Control and Prevention says the percentage of adults aged eighteen and over who met the Physical Activity Guidelines for both aerobic and muscle-strengthening activity is 23.2 percent.[16]

That means a lot of us do not see this as a priority. Sure, the importance of exercise to health is well known and documented, so here are some benefit reminders to you from the Mayo Clinic.[16]

- Controls weight
- Combats health conditions and diseases
- Improves your mood
- Boosts energy
- Promotes better sleep
- Puts a spark back in your sex life
- Can be fun and social

While I suggest the primary motive for exercise should be your general health, I also want to show you through the PEC of *exercise time optimization* why this will benefit your overall productivity. Using the Mayo Clinic list . . . improving your mood, boosting energy, and promoting better sleep are the three categories directly tied to helping shift time from managed to optimized.

EXERCISE: PREPARATION

The frequency and duration around the benefits of exercise are pretty consistent. All healthy adults aged eighteen to sixty-five years should participate in moderate-intensity aerobic physical activity for a minimum of thirty minutes, five days per week, or vigorous-intensity aerobic activity for a minimum of twenty minutes, three days per week.[18] That equates to about 150 minutes a week. Assuming you sleep eight hours a night (I know, a stretch for many of us) that leaves 6,720 minutes of time you are awake each week. A committed physical activity plan takes only 2.2 percent of your awake time.

Following an adage from a mentor of mine to "never fail to state the obvious," preparation here is not telling you the right equipment to buy (though, that is important), doing the right stretches (that reduces injury), or eating right (that helps your endurance). Seek the right advice from the right subject matter experts. I would suggest a visit to your doctor if you are starting from scratch.

There are reams of information about the right time of day to work out. Factors include weight, physical condition, age, and general health. For the purposes of time optimization, we will follow the philosophy of "the best time to exercise is whenever you can."[19] Look at your calendar and get it on there as a formal event. Even add exercise as a reoccurring task that reminds you as a to-do that it needs to be done.

EXERCISE: EXECUTION

To *execute*, you need to start, so start. To stay committed to the process, do things that positively motivate you to keep going.

- Monitor your progress
- Keep what you do interesting
- Overcome the disruptions to your routine
- Be flexible in that routine
- Know where to get help and support[20]

Life will seek to crowd out this time. Remember, you are only asking yourself to spend about 2 percent of your waking hours to exercise. Remind yourself and execute against that, even if you set an interim goal of ninety minutes or about 1 percent of awake time a week.

EXERCISE: CONTROL

If exercising during the times you have scheduled does not happen consistently, then establish some goals based on your type of exercise. Maintain control by pushing yourself to meet those objectives.

Exercise time optimization almost merges execution and control together. The key to control is patience. Results from exercise do not come quickly or easily, particularly the older you get. Go back to preparation and ask yourself three questions.

- Since starting to exercise, has my mood improved?
- Do I have more energy during the day because I exercise?
- Am I sleeping better because I worked out?

Given enough time, you will see yourself answering yes to one or all of them.

JULIE'S EXERCISE

Like with Dr. Divya Jaitly, Julie and I have never met in person. However, without trying to sound weird, she looks healthy on screen. Upon asking her why she exercises so well, Julie responded, "Being in the military you learn, even though I did not want to get up, I was pushing myself much further than I would have, normally. You then realize you just feel great the rest of the day. When it is done, you still feel amazing."

However, she also credits her family life growing up. Her mom set a great example. As a schoolteacher, she would jog during the lunch breaks to help keep her energy up. Her grandmother also walked everywhere and never drove.

Julie has a diverse workout routine. "I used to be a pretty passionate runner and did a lot of half-marathons. Now I am trying to be more balanced, so I do less running and more walking, yoga, and Pilates."

By being committed to exercise, she feels she is a much happier and more alert person. She sleeps better and is much more rested to take on challenges. "It just makes everything function better."

Her advice to others is to have at least three one-hour sessions a week (slightly higher than the CDC average but still less than 3 percent of your awake time). If you can't do that, then at least get in a twenty-minute walk per day. For those who travel, make sure to exercise and be careful about what you eat if you can't workout.

SPIRITUALITY

I have not hidden my spiritual beliefs in this book. My Christian faith has provided me with some amazing *kairos* moments. As noted in the Introduction, *kairos* times are those instances of joy, frustration, satisfaction, determination, resolution, and completion. You may not be able to quantify the time that was expended, but the time it took can have a deep and long-lasting emotional impact.

So much of my spiritual journey revolves around gratitude to God and to the others He has put in my path. As my wife, the Rev. Dr. Susan Rose, has stated in her blog:

> *Having a practice of gratitude has [been] shown to have all kinds of benefits such as boosting mental health, relieving stress, and helping to accept change. We can practice gratitude as a solo practice or express our gratitude to or with others. Either way, may we give thanks to God for the big and small things in our daily lives that are good.*[21]

The manner of spirituality from a time optimization view still has elements of PEC, but they are very personal and can be unique for the individual.

SPIRITUALITY: PREPARATION

From a tactical standpoint, spirituality requires preparation. Using this book as a guide, time could be invested and shown on your calendar and/or task list. There could be moments of prayer, reading Scripture, attending your place of worship, and other relegated community activities tied to your faith. They can be tangible to you because you see them taking up space and time.

SPIRITUALITY: EXECUTION

Spiritual execution can take many forms. Prayer, meditation, and quiet moments require an investment of time. Attendance at a physical place of worship or an event could demand multiple steps of planning. I know on some Sundays, just getting our family to church on time seemed like a herculean effort. Getting deeper into your experience may force you to make time-management choices.

SPIRITUALITY: CONTROL

Spiritual control is directly proportionate to the effort you expend. My Christian journey has been populated with numerous high and low points. When spirituality became a lower priority in my life, I found I lost control of time—or, more truthfully, I let control be lost. The more a spiritual path is important it is to you, the more the religion or practice crowds out other, less important activities.

Back in Chapter 1, I talked about the various approaches different worldviews have about the passage of time. Whether your spirituality is linear, cyclical, illusionary, or varied, the clock still moves forward as we all share this existence. You can't control the passage of time, but you can control your engagement. If spirituality is important to you, then formalize it into your time optimization plan.

Trait	Preparation	Execution	Control
Sleep	Plan for 8 hours.	Be good at it.	Be intentional.
Breaks	Find your zone.	Have a productive break.	Start small and build.
Exercise	Reserve 2% of your time.	Stay motivated.	Be patient.
Spirituality	Make it tangible to your schedule.	Make spiritual choices.	Don't get lost.

FIGURE 8:3 PERSONAL CARE TIME-OPTIMIZED SUMMARY

A LITTLE REMINDER

As I have mentioned throughout the book, my wife has played a pivotal role in my life. The Reverend Doctor Susan Rose has positively impacted my time-optimized journey in so many ways. Now, as promised, I am turning over the book to her. Chapter 9 is fully her perspective and her voice, showing you that PEC can be used in different ways. I will see you back in Chapter 10.

CHAPTER 9

Susan Rose,
Another Time-Optimized Perspective

Setting unrealistic expectations of yourself—of your time and
your well-being—doesn't lead to time optimization. It leads
to exhaustion. I don't think anyone has set exhaustion as a life goal,
yet we set our schedules up as if it is our top priority.
(Rev. Dr. Susan Rose)

Dave is the hardest-working, most disciplined man I know.

I understand I come to this statement with some bias, being his wife of almost thirty years.

When he decided to write *The Time-Optimized Life*, based on his organizational system that contributed to his high level of success in the business world, I had no doubt he would do it. In our conversations surrounding the book, I quipped that a chapter should be dedicated to time management from a woman's perspective. When he negotiated the publishing contract, that idea, still yet-to-be-written, was an aspect that intrigued the publisher.

Dave intentionally highlights women from different backgrounds who excel in particular aspects of time management in the book. I think their stories strengthen the book. Their diverse backgrounds transcend the idea that time-management principles belong to men in middle and upper management. Adhering to their time-management practices and strengths contributes to the success of each of the women in their personal and professional lives.

My idea of suggesting a chapter from a woman's perspective of time management came from my experience. I read and followed time-management experts, predominately men, who would share their weekly calendars to show how high levels of productivity could be achieved. As I viewed those calendars, not one of them ever remotely reflected my life and schedule, or those of many of my female professional friends.

The "calendars from the experts" reflect complete control over their time. One of the aspects that are key to a productive day is their morning rituals. They get up and do their morning routine: meditation/devotional time/journaling, workout, shower/change, and arrive at their desks at a set time to begin their days. For working women with children, this schedule reflects a retreat, not a daily routine.

Women often don't have the luxury of taking care of just themselves before heading to work. Where are the kids? There is no mention of the morning hustle and bustle of getting children up, fed, and out the door—or driving carpool—with lunch and all appropriate papers and assignments in hand or bag.

What's for dinner, and who is taking care of it, including shopping and preparation? Do they have pets? Who feeds them, walks them, cleans up after them? What about scheduling household things when something breaks, then coordinating schedules to meet them at the house?

This was the morning routine that reflected my life for close to twenty years. *Then* I went to work and school.

The set afternoon schedules of the calendar experts didn't reflect my life either, with neatly blocked time until 5 or 6 p.m. In my reality, afternoon schedules were another version of busyness, depending on the children's activities, school events, and life events. Again, time-management experts never revealed household tasks on their calendars—activities like grocery shopping, cooking, cleaning, running errands, and attending vet appointments or doctors' appointments. That meant that someone, either paid or unpaid, was getting this all done so they could be productive in their professional and personal time. I was always going to fail at that kind of time management because it didn't reflect my actual lived experience.

A 2019 Gallup poll reflected that married women still do more of the household chores than their husbands.[1] However, the statistics show a narrowing of the gap between gender and the division of labor at home. A study conducted between 2015–2017 showed that even when women were the primary income earners, housework and childcare averaged 43.4 hours a week, compared to 30.3 hours for their husbands.[2] If a woman is working full-time, she's working an eighty-hour week combined between professional and personal schedules. If her husband is the breadwinner, the average hours of combined housework and childcare rise to 55.1 hours a week. That means if she's working part-time for twenty hours a week, she's clocking in seventy-five hours a week.[3]

One of the most interesting articles I uncovered in my research was a transcript from an NPR interview on *All Things Considered*. In it, Eve Rodsky says the gap between women, men, and household chores is attributed to how we think about time. She says, "As a society, we've chosen to view and value men's time as if it's diamonds and finite, and we've chosen to value women's time as if it's infinite like sand."[4] She reminds us that everyone gets twenty-four hours in a day. Equally valuing each other's time and daily communication is key to closing the gap.

What I want to say to women in this chapter is "I see you" and "I understand" when time management is one more thing that doesn't measure up to a standard someone else sets for you.

I am not going to tell you "if only" you will follow my way—or Dave's way—it will solve all your time-management problems. That was my biggest issue with time-management experts: my life's schedule could never conform to their system. I "failed" before even beginning.

Having a time-management system is important. Imperative even. However, when you are tasked with "all other duties as required but not enumerated," often the systems don't work because they simply don't reflect the reality of women's lived experiences. I am encouraging you to develop your own system of *preparation*, *execution*, and *control*. As I continue to share my story in this chapter, you will see that I utilize the PEC principles in a completely different way than Dave uses them. The principles remain the same. How they are implemented is unique to my needs.

Dave and I have had a somewhat traditional marriage in that he worked full-time while I stayed home with our children. "Staying home" is a bit of a misnomer, since I almost always worked part-time, went to school for advanced degrees, and managed the house. It is also important to note that managing the house for me is different from the term "housekeeping." I hate to clean. Dave loves to clean. At some point early in our relationship, he took on the vast majority of cleaning on Saturdays. Our boys will tell you that they also did quite a bit of cleaning, as well as yardwork. It was an all-hands-on-deck activity. My role in cleaning was narrowed to something I could manage, like cleaning bathrooms and doing laundry.

However, the vast majority of the "rest of the stuff" about running the house and our lives fell to me. I am not complaining about our life or our marriage. We have been incredibly fortunate, even in the worst of times. We have achieved this because of our faith and our teamwork. We worked as a team to achieve our goals—*together*. Sometimes this looked very "traditional." A lot of times, it was not traditional at all. Working together to achieve our goals, small or big, was just how we grew in our marriage.

But my calendar, my time, was never exclusively *mine*. Even now, as an empty nester, participating more in the care of my mother means that my schedule accommodates events that are often unplanned.

Dave has been honest with the difference between our organizational systems throughout the book. I hate to file. I always have. Hence, I developed an exceptional ability to know where items were in the midst of my piles. Dave files everything, but as he has noted, sometimes we have to go through several iterations to find *where* an item might be filed. I have dubbed this process, "Think like Dave." In moments of frustration, I will actually calm myself down and do my best to *think like Dave* . . . and I can normally find whatever I'm looking for much more quickly.

I shared with you earlier that Dave and I have different approaches to time optimization. He is all electronic. I'm all paper. His system works for him. He has used it for years. It allows him to achieve goals and accomplish myriad tasks in multiple business settings. But it doesn't fit my life and my career. I handle preparation, execution, and control differently.

MY CALENDAR PEC

I initially started working with an electronic calendar in the early days of having an iPhone. As a pastor, I would get requests to speak or preach or attend events in addition to my "regular" pastoring duties. I would look at my phone, and it would have "dots" on the days that I had made commitments. However, the dot wouldn't tell me what I had committed *to*. I reverted to a paper calendar after one particularly horrible preparation, execution, and control week. I had agreed to attend an all-day Saturday event *and* preach on Sunday, on top of a full week in my "regular" ministry job. I left myself no time for good preaching preparation. I also did not leave myself any downtime, or Sabbath. In that particular season of life, I was still working under the misguided impression that I could sleep when I was dead. I made it through the over-scheduling snafus, but I determined I needed to "see" my week and month to not do that again.

I'd like to point out that this spiral of poor preparation, execution, and control is a pattern of behavior that we get stuck in. This pattern doesn't have to be your normal. Setting unrealistic expectations of yourself—of your time and your well-being—doesn't lead to time optimization. It leads to exhaustion. I don't think anyone has set exhaustion as a life goal, yet we set our schedules up as if it is our top priority. Again, I encourage you to embrace a form of PEC that works for you and your goals.

I went through a couple of years of creating my own calendar. I did not like what was on the market, so I created my weekly calendar based on how I needed to view and plan my schedule. This was my "grids" stage. I hand-wrote my calendar on graph paper for a month (or a semester) at a time. While Dave pointed out that this was not an efficient use of my time, I found a bit of "Zen" in the art of its creation. Sometimes, I used colored pens. There was something reflective about the writing out of my schedule. I enjoyed that phase of my calendaring journey.

As I changed jobs and life phases, I changed my approach to calendaring again. I set broader goals in time blocks, with a list of tasks that needed to be accomplished in the margins. That worked for a season as well, up to and through the pandemic.

As we emerged from the pandemic, I switched calendars once more. I flirted with an online calendar again. As I launched my nonprofit, I attempted to work with an electronic calendar because of my work with individual clients. This time, my progress was thwarted for several reasons. First, anything tech-related is difficult for me. Remember when Dave said he devoted several weeks to becoming an expert at Excel in its early days? He will still watch YouTube videos on Excel and take specialized classes to enhance his knowledge. He really loves it. He also has the patience to learn new tech skills in the evenings and on weekends. (Remember, he is incredibly disciplined when he wants to achieve a goal.) I am not tech-adept in that way. I don't have the patience for it. I don't want to spend my downtime learning new tech skills. Furthermore, if something bizarre can go wrong with me and tech, it will. Dave can attest to this.

Second, as someone who is bivocational, working several part-time jobs in ministry, there are times when I may have time blocked for one job, but another job requires immediate attention. As a pastor, this is often in the form of a pastoral need or crisis. After a few weeks of spending more time rearranging my time and availability, I simply took the calendar link down. It doesn't work for this phase of my career.

Dave rightly points out that I may need to revisit using an electronic calendar if I reach scale in my nonprofit. He is right. But right now, I neither have the capacity nor the patience to embrace a new way of planning my time. So I'm old-school, using a paper calendar. Again. It is how I best use PEC to achieve my goals.

Finally, my job—or jobs—is about being relational. Can I do a better job of maintaining boundaries? Sure I can. This is something I continually need to practice: being available but still setting boundaries to achieve what I need to do that day, week, or month. It's a growing edge for me.

TIME-MANAGEMENT DIETING

Sometimes, time management becomes like dieting. When I slip up, instead of acknowledging the "slip" and returning to a disciplined routine, I throw everything out the window and eat the entire cake. I actually never have eaten an entire cake. But you understand the point. If you can't execute the calendar or time management (or diet) perfectly, then what's the point of doing *any* of it? That all-or-nothing thinking may last for a week or two, or even a season, but eventually, I come back to the discipline and routine of calendaring . . . and eating well. It just works better for me.

Perfectionism is a key component of "all-or-nothing" thinking. I think a lot of women have an inner critic, encouraged by society and social media, that tells them perfection is the standard and anything less is failure. One author puts it this way: "Something has to be perfect or it's not good enough."[5] Working harder and striving more is not the answer. Remember, exhaustion is not the goal. Living your best time-optimized kairos life is. Resetting and reevaluating your situation to move forward appropriately is a good first step.

Accepting "good enough" is especially difficult if you hold yourself to unrealistic expectations. Dave traveled for his job throughout our marriage, until the pandemic. When the kids were growing up, he would be on the road every week or every other week for work. One of those weeks he was out of town, after-school activities ran late. I was pulling into the garage around 6 p.m. We were all *hangry*. Whatever I had planned for dinner was not going to happen. I remember sighing, feeling defeated, and thinking I was not going to be able to make my children "a good dinner." This was one of those self-imposed standards I had put on myself related to being "a good mother." As I put the car in park, I said, "OK, boys, you can have cereal for dinner, and I'll make smoothies." You know what my children said? In unison, they yelled, "This is the best night EVER!" Hmmmm . . . all those years, I twisted myself into knots to make a good dinner when we could have been having cereal one night a week when Dad was traveling?! Good enough is good enough. Give yourself some grace and move on.

SOLVING THE CALENDAR CRISIS

So what do I do when my schedule gets blown up?

For me, it begins before the calendar crisis. This would be the preparation phase within PEC. As a reminder, Dave defines time-optimized time management as the "continuous pursuit of the right preparation, along with the right execution, to escalate broad control over personal productivity." I've learned that I do better with disruptions and calendar challenges when I've spent time grounding myself for the day in silence, Scripture, and prayer. Some days, this unfolds at an easy pace. Some days, it's a quick, git-'er-done practice. Some days, it's a prayer app that I listen to in the car on the way to where I need to be. And some days, I just blow through the practice altogether. You see, even as an empty nester and, in theory, completely in charge of my schedule, some days just go sideways. That's OK.

These are spiritual practices that help *me* stay grounded. *You* may find other practices, spiritual or not, work better for you. And if you don't know what works for you, challenge yourself for a month or two to "try on" different practices for a week at a time. Each person is unique, and each season of life has its own set of demands. Find what works for you. If and when a practice no longer works, explore a new practice. It's perfectly fine to adapt to new—and different—circumstances.

When my calendar gets re-arranged, I reflect, even for a split second, on my practice for that day as I move forward with changes. This helps me navigate the changes with a sense of calm and peace. I reprioritize as necessary. I remember to be graceful with myself. And sometimes, I call or text a friend to vent my frustration. Then I move forward. Some items get re-arranged. Some items get dropped. And sometimes, I end up working in the evenings or on weekends to catch up. It all depends upon the goals for the week and the nature of the interruption. I continue to confront the tyranny of "perfection or failure" with my calendar and my goals. I continue to work on being more graceful with myself and accepting good enough as good enough when scheduling goes awry. Practicing (and implementing) preparation, execution, and control looks different for me than for Dave, but the principles remain the same.

This is where I set aside the chronos mindset and lean into the kairos mindset. Maybe it's the perspective of age and experience that has shaped my embrace of kairos time. I recognize I don't have an endless supply of energy or time. Overworking has consequences: I can work a long day (or days) and forgo downtime and the Sabbath, but there will be a cost to me. Ultimately, I find I am *less* productive and *less* focused.

Life experience and perspective have also taught me the preciousness of kairos time. I spent a good part of my life chasing tomorrow and not enjoying today. What I'm doing, and with whom, impacts how I prioritize my time now. This is my PEC journey. I try to execute chronos time well to spend more of my life in kairos time.

How will you spend your chronos time to live in your kairos time?

CHAPTER 10

The Time-Optimized Life

There is a time for everything,
*   and a season for every activity under the heavens:*
a time to be born and a time to die,
*   a time to plant and a time to uproot,*
a time to kill and a time to heal,
*   a time to tear down and a time to build,*
a time to weep and a time to laugh,
*   a time to mourn and a time to dance,*
a time to scatter stones and a time to gather them,
*   a time to embrace and a time to refrain from embracing,*
a time to search and a time to give up,
*   a time to keep and a time to throw away,*
a time to tear and a time to mend,
*   a time to be silent and a time to speak,*
a time to love and a time to hate,
*   a time for war and a time for peace* (Ecclesiastes 3:1–8).

his passage noted from the Book of Ecclesiastes in the Bible is very popular. If there are any 1960s Rock & Roll music fans reading this, you might know the lyrics to the song by The Byrd's titled, "Turn! Turn! Turn!" that was released in 1965.

Obviously, there are significant references to time from the Scripture referenced above. Notice the word *time* is used around constant action. A decision or motion is tied to each verse. The same applies to your approach to the use of your time. Let's remind ourselves of the definition again.

> *Time Optimized* **time management is a continuous pursuit of the right** *preparation*, **along with the right** *execution*, **to escalate broad** *control* **over personal productivity.**

From everything presented to you in Chapters 1–9, it can be hard to know where to start. Let me set some expectations upfront. When you read the last page and close the cover of the book, nothing will change in your life unless you choose to act.

As I noted at the close of Chapter 3, now is the time to be a TOP, time-optimized planner.

I have read (and referenced) a lot of great business manuscripts throughout the writing of this book. Only a few can I say made a significant contribution to improving my life. It is not because of the content of their books (far from it); it is because I failed to or decided not to take the great advice that was given and make it a reality by investing the time needed to impact my life.

One positive example for me is *Death by Meeting* (quoted a couple of times in this book). After finishing it, I made a strong effort to implement the principles Patrick Lencioni presented. Introducing one type called the "Daily Stand-up" meeting to the members of my team was awkward and uncomfortable. Many times, I felt like giving up, but after a time, it became ingrained in the culture and developed into a useful and time-beneficial practice. To this day, I still use the premise behind the types and durations of gatherings offered in *Death by Meeting*.

Should this book you are reading be worthy of an additional investment of your time, what follows in this chapter will be an outline you can structure to a pattern I present, or you can create a fully customized model to your taste and needs. A time-optimized life will only become a reality when you commit to investing the time in what may already be a time-challenged time in your life.

While I have yet to find someone who has difficulty with everything, there are plenty of people who struggle with a lot of the sections in the book. PEC is woven throughout. Preparation, execution, and control are the three points of the productivity triangle, continuously used to improve your efficiency and yield. They are the three points to the time-optimized life.

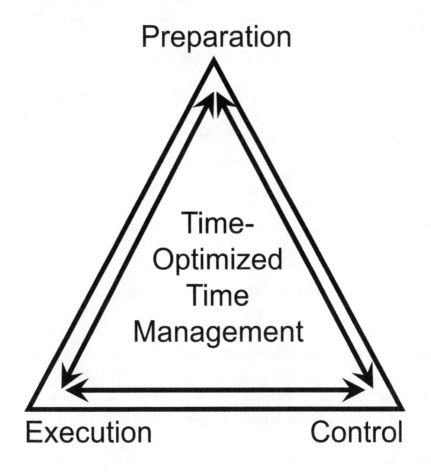

FIGURE 10:1 TIME-OPTIMIZED TIME MANAGEMENT

Therefore, you guessed it, in this last chapter, we will use PEC to help you craft the right approach that works for you.

The first action will be *Strategy Preparation*. For clients of Kairos Management Solutions, the start of their time-optimized development begins with the Time Management Analysis (TMA). I have referenced this assessment a lot, and for those who have taken it, you see that this book is an extension of the tool itself.

Planning	Task Management	Internal Focus	External Focus	Organization	Personal Care
Goals	Having a List	Procrastination	Talking	Finishing	Sleep
Mapping Ahead	Prioritization	Motivation	Interruptions	Calendar	Breaks
Meetings	Multitasking	Distractions	Saying "No"	Organized	Exercise
Assignments					Spirituality

10:2 THE 5 CATEGORIES AND 20 SECTIONS OF TIME OPTIMIZATION PRESENTED IN ORDER

The simplest outline of the book can be seen in Figure 10:2. Time optimization consists of six categories (really five, but we broke focus into two distinct types) and twenty sections. As you look at it, you can probably identify which ones represent your strengths and weaknesses. There could be entire categories that need your attention or simply certain sections. If you want to reset, revamp, or just look to wipe the slate clean and build new time-optimized ways, this is the area for you. We will walk through a strategy based on the data collected and analyzed from all the participants of the TMA. You can adapt it to suit your needs and lifestyle.

Moving to the *E* in PEC, *Strategy Execution* lays out the way in which you will live the tactics established in the strategy. We did not introduce new and fancy tools in this book. Between a calendar, a solid task-management program, and your grit and determination, you have the means to deliver amazing personal results that will also positively impact those around you.

The hardest part of PEC is *Strategy Control*. There is a difference between being busy and being productive. I recently had a conversation with a client who was trying to figure out the next major step in her life.

"I could fill up my calendar with stuff very quickly, but I don't just want to be doing stuff. I want to be doing things with meaning and purpose," she said.

That is the difference between wanting to be busy and wanting to be productive. Your exercise of time-optimized strategy control is to recognize and push back against those demands that move you off or delay your goals. What you plan in strategy preparation is going to change. Again, PEC is about action and movement.

The time-optimized personalities that were featured in this book all have unique approaches. Matt Anselmo has a personal PEC that relies heavily on execution and control because events in his life can change quickly. Tracy Holmes enjoys the preparation but thrives in the control phase. Julie Blacutt also likes to prepare but has a desire to execute strongly. Ellie Buck, because she is so organized, is immersed in preparation that eases the burden of execution and control. Hunter Camp has such a demanding vocation that he highly covets control to maintain the best work-life balance. Divya Jaitly has a strategic mindset geared toward the future but must continuously control her efforts, given the demands of her time.

Wherever you land, make it your own PEC. Rely on your strengths to develop your weaknesses.

STRATEGY: PREPARATION

If you are still not sure where to start, then I am going to do a little self-promotion here.

As a reader of this book, I am offering you the opportunity to take the Time Management Analysis (TMA) for free. Head to the resource page right after this chapter and find the website address for the TMA. Answer all twenty of the scenarios, and you'll receive your personalized, detailed report within forty-eight hours.

After doing that, you can come right back here and have the blueprint you need to lay out the plan. For the rest of you who are thinking, "I am almost done with the book, he better not stop now," no need to worry. I am honored that you have invested the time, and you certainly can move forward with or without the TMA.

There are different ways to tackle your strategy preparation.

Priority Category Prioritization uses the data compiled from the TMA directly and will provide you with a structured disposition to follow in your efforts. *Self-Selecting Sections* uses a personal ranking system where you choose the units to work on first, using a priority method. When you have reached a comfort level, then you introduce another section to provide focus. Finally, *Potpourri Sections* is less about establishing priorities, more about aligning which units to tackle based on personal and professional considerations. Again, all these can be implemented by having taken the TMA or with a blank canvas.

PRIORITY CATEGORY PRIORITIZATION

The Time Management Analysis uses an index system between 0 and 100. The index ranks individuals into four classifications, shown in Figure 10:3. The percentage notes the number of participants who scored in that specific category.

Category	Description
Time Talented 7.5%	A Time-Talented person successfully manages their time. They effectively use tools to assist in their planning. Talented time managers meet deadlines. Through limiting interruptions and not procrastinating, they have the ability to stay focused. It is important for them to maintain a healthy lifestyle.
Time Inclusive 32.2%	For a Time-Inclusive person, time management is a formal routine. They try to incorporate tools to assist their planning. They meet deadlines frequently but can get distracted. Interruptions and procrastination can hinder their ability to focus. They try to maintain a healthy lifestyle.
Time Modest 40.0%	Time-Modest individuals can plan well but may not tie that back to time management. They work on organization but will lose focus when there are a lot of activities to be completed. There is uneven task execution. Personal care and health are inconsistent and may not be areas of emphasis.
Time Expand 20.4%	Time-Expand people rarely have a formal plan or process in place. They are very reactive and often feel under pressure. Deadlines are frequently missed, and they struggle to be ready for meetings. Focus is difficult because of outside interruptions, distractions, and demands.

FIGURE 10:3 CLASSIFICATIONS OF THE TIME MANAGEMENT ANALYSIS

The average person falls in the *Time Modest* classification. Using that as our foundation and applying the same process to each priority category, we establish the outline shown in Figure 10:2 to reflect the priority categories from the lowest to the highest index. The smaller the index, the higher the priority to work to improve. Now the plan would look like Figure 10:4.

Priority Category Prioritization Execution Outline					
(1) Personal Care	(2) Internal Focus	(3) External Focus	(4) Task Management	(5) Planning	(6) Organization
(1) Sleep	(1) Procrastination	(1) Interruptions	(1) Multitasking	(1) Goals	(1) Organized
(2) Exercise	(2) Distractions	(2) Saying "No"	(2) Prioritization	(2) Mapping Ahead	(2) Calendar
(3) Breaks	(3) Motivation	(3) Talking	(3) Having a List	(3) Assignment	(3) Finishing
(4) Spirituality				(4) Meetings	

FIGURE 10:4: PRIORITY CATEGORY PRIORITIZATION EXECUTION OUTLINE

This is the framework to form your time optimization strategy from scratch. Depending on your comfort level and urgency, you can choose to "walk and chew gum" at the same time. For example, you can start *Personal Care* and *Internal Focus* together, since an activity like sleep does not conflict with distractions that might happen in the day. Let's walk through each category.

From the TMA data, *Personal Care* is the biggest area for improvement and, hopefully, the easiest time-optimized way to get started. Of that, the place to get underway is your ability to have more sleep. The goal is between seven and nine hours. Give your mind and body the rest it requires to have the energy during the day to apply to other areas. Harder to get consistent, exercise also assists and raises both strength and spirit. Reset your brain and open the opportunity for creativity and vitality by taking formal breaks. While spirituality is very personal, creating a deeper connection to it may unlock a desire to see time differently. Refer to Chapter 8 for the details of your essentials.

Directly tied to your professional and personal life, *Internal Focus* comes in as a close second to *Personal Care*. Your attention here is on you. No excuses. Break the rut of procrastination to keep forward movement. Create an environment that limits you from getting distracted. See how to check your motivation so that you are positively looking for time-optimized behaviors. Jump back to Chapter 5 and see what you can apply to your plan.

Not surprisingly, *External Focus* comes next. Focus is a broad topic, which is why there are two segments dedicated to it in this book. As you refresh yourself with Chapter 6, insulate yourself from distractions, and make sure you pay attention to the impact of interruptions. Saying no requires anticipating constructive responses because of a well-planned schedule highlighted in your task list and calendar. There is no "gift of gab" in time optimization. If the talk is not productive, understand how you can stop it so you can get back to accomplishing your goals.

A *to-do list* is indispensable. Deciding on the optimal task-management program is an entryway to so many ways of time improvement. Keep yourself out of the multitasking trap. Know what is important and prioritize what needs to be done. Having a well-established list rounds out what we covered in detail in Chapter 4.

Planning has a lot of elements. Personal goals are often overlooked; in fact, 42 percent of those taking the TMA have informal or no objectives and aspirations planned. Reserve dedicated time on goals, and revisit the types in Chapter 3 if needed. Mapping ahead and completing assignments are mindset exercises that need constant attention and care. Finally, because we spend so much time in meetings, seek to treat them as time-optimized openings and not a drag on your morale and productivity.

Just because *Organization* is listed last, does not mean it should be ignored. Knowing where to find what you need, when you need it, is the definition of being organized. That can take more time than you think to formulate. I have stated my passion for the calendar. This is the single most important time optimization tool. Take the attempt to allocate the proper intervals of effort. To repeat what I said back in Chapter 7, when you engage in the preparation of finishing, it is because you are having a problem with the PEC of an already established project or task. To get good at this requires you to be observant of your efficiency.

Remember, start *Personal Care* and one other category. If you do not have a personal care issue, then attempt one category at a time, even only one section at a time. This is the *P* of PEC; until you can prove you can execute and control, the less you take on the better.

SELF-SELECTING SECTIONS

Should this section look like your method to use for preparation, I will ask you to go back and read the four classifications in Figure 10:3. If either *Modest* or *Inclusive* seems to be the best fit for your current state, great—you are in the right place. If *Expand* seems more like your self-diagnosis, seriously consider the broader and comprehensive approach in the previous section. However, you can still use the self-select process; time optimization will not be denied you with consistent effort. A *Talented* person should stay here and complete the exercise, but the next area fits even better because of the solid skills shown in many of the priority category sections.

Instead of using the assessment from the Time Management Analysis report (though, please take advantage of the free offer in the Resources section after this chapter), here you will apply a basic version of the TMA. Figure 10:5 is the template you can use to customize your approach.

Using the previous chapters as a reference, rate yourself on each of the twenty sections, using the 1 to 10 scale. Mark on the low end if you consider yourself a *novice*. As a learner, you seek the fundamentals. On the other end of the scale, being an *expert* means you are knowledgeable and skilled—not really seeing a need for any improvement. Circle your designations, add up the total score for the category, and write it down.

Category	Section	Novice									Expert	Average
Planning	Goals	1	2	3	4	5	6	7	8	9	10	Planning Score
	Mapping Ahead	1	2	3	4	5	6	7	8	9	10	
	Meetings	1	2	3	4	5	6	7	8	9	10	
	Assignment	1	2	3	4	5	6	7	8	9	10	_____
Task Management	Having a List	1	2	3	4	5	6	7	8	9	10	Task Management Score
	Prioritization	1	2	3	4	5	6	7	8	9	10	
	Multitasking (Not)	1	2	3	4	5	6	7	8	9	10	_____
Internal Focus	Procrastination	1	2	3	4	5	6	7	8	9	10	Internal Focus Score
	Motivation	1	2	3	4	5	6	7	8	9	10	
	Distractions	1	2	3	4	5	6	7	8	9	10	_____
External Focus	Talking	1	2	3	4	5	6	7	8	9	10	External Focus Score
	Interruptions	1	2	3	4	5	6	7	8	9	10	
	Saying "No"	1	2	3	4	5	6	7	8	9	10	_____
Organization	Finishing	1	2	3	4	5	6	7	8	9	10	Organization Score
	Calendar	1	2	3	4	5	6	7	8	9	10	
	Organized	1	2	3	4	5	6	7	8	9	10	_____
Personal Care	Sleep	1	2	3	4	5	6	7	8	9	10	Personal Care Score
	Breaks	1	2	3	4	5	6	7	8	9	10	
	Exercise	1	2	3	4	5	6	7	8	9	10	
	Spirituality	1	2	3	4	5	6	7	8	9	10	_____

FIGURE 10:5 SELF-SELECTING THE SECTIONS FOR IMPROVEMENT

Many of you are calling me out right now for my process. "But Dave, Personal Care and Planning each have four sections while the others have three. That will give me the wrong ranking."

Yes, you are correct, which is why you need to do a little more math. Take the total of that category and divide it by the number of sections in that category to get an average score. Another little plug here, the TMA does all the math for you (visit the References section). Record that number in the average column.

By now, there should be some variance between each of the categories. Your plan ought to start with the lowest average score.

Within that category, your tactics begin with the lowest-scored section. Using the example in Figure 10:6, your Internal Focus methodology starts with procrastination, moves to distractions, then to motivation. Should you self-rate at a nine or ten in any particular unit, and if you feel you have mastered the other sections, move to the next category; come back later if you desire to fine-tune that particular item.

Category	Section	Novice							Expert			Average
	Procrastination	1	2	③	4	5	6	7	8	9	10	Internal Focus Score
Internal Focus	Motivation	1	2	3	4	5	6	7	⑧	9	10	
	Distractions	1	2	3	④	5	6	7	8	9	10	**5.0**

FIGURE 10:6 INTERNAL FOCUS SELF-SELECT EXAMPLE

Congrats, you have now established a solid outline to begin executing your strategy!

POTPOURRI SECTIONS

Noting that less than one in ten are designated as *Time Talented* from the TMA results, this section is the place for you. Some within the *Time Inclusive* group may also like this method. Just like what was reviewed in the self-selecting process, go back to Figure 10:5 and self-assess on each section. Instead of looking at the average score for each category, you drill down to the section ranking, starting with the lowest score.

For the *Time Modest* and *Expand* folks, you may like this method as well. Be careful about staying focused. The sections within a category are designed to complement one another. Jumping from section to section in different categories may produce inconsistent results.

Regardless of your strategy preparation choice, go at preparation with a purpose. Give yourself the opportunity to succeed. Heck, set these as personal goals (Chapter 3), get them laid out on your calendar (Chapter 7), and set tasks daily (Chapter 4) to help monitor progress. Be committed and focused (Chapters 5 and 6). Prepare yourself to execute and control your time optimization improvement.

STRATEGY: EXECUTION

Please, do not expect results overnight. A single night of eight hours of sleep is not a trend. One week of planning your calendar is not a habit. Getting all your tasks done on time for five days straight is not a permanent accomplishment. Patience please, patience. Before you read this book, I imagine most of you have functioned at some level of capability and that your world was not a total chaotic mess around you. As the results show from the TMA, most people have targeted areas for improvement and other areas where they do well. Those high-functioning categories and sections get used over and over to compensate for the challenge areas. Time optimization seeks to raise all of them to a *Time-Talented* status.

Therefore, you want to take one or two, maybe even three sections, and work those to become habits. That may sound like a dirty word to some of you; we all have habits already. Charles Duhigg in his excellent book, *The Power of Habit*, describes it this way:

> *Habits, scientists say, emerge because the brain is constantly looking for ways to save effort. Left to its own devices, the brain will try to make any routine into a habit, because habit allows our minds to ramp down more often. The [effort-saving] instinct is a huge advantage. An efficient brain also allows us to stop thinking constantly about basic behaviors such as walking and choosing what we eat, so we can devote mental energy to inventing spears, irrigation systems, and, eventually airplanes and video games.*[1]

Thinking along these lines, wherever you choose to execute your time optimization, introduce sections into your day as routines, formally established and visible, on your calendar or task list. As Tracy Holmes noted back in Chapter 3, create a vision board as a reminder of what you are trying to accomplish and put it in a place to remind yourself of its contents.

PRIORITY CATEGORY: EXECUTION

Applying the more formal approach outlined in Figure 10:4, and based on the averages established in the TMA responses, Priority Category Execution plays off the scenarios and set into Figure 10:5. The program starts with *Personal Care* and weaves its way down to *Organization*. Obviously, there is room for customization. You may already have a great exercise regimen; therefore, there is no need to execute against that.

Category	Section	Start Date	Targeted 8 to 10 Scale Date	Actual 8 to 10 Scale Date
Personal Care	Sleep			
	Exercise			
	Breaks			
	Spirituality			
Internal Focus	Procrastination			
	Distractions			
	Motivation			
External Focus	Interruptions			
	Saying "No"			
	Talking			
Task Management	Multitasking (Not)			
	Having a List			
	Prioritization			
Planning	Goals			
	Mapping Ahead			
	Assignments			
	Meetings			
Organization	Organized			
	Calendar			
	Finishing			

FIGURE 10:7 ESTABLISHING TIME-OPTIMIZED TIMELINES

Using the Time-Optimized Task Design discussed in Chapter 4, take a selected section, and set a task with a "Targeted 8 to 10 Scale Date." That term is the date when you think you'll be able to self-evaluate your performance at an eight or above (see Figure 10:5).

Unfortunately, I cannot tell you how long it will take for you to turn a section from a challenge into a time-optimized benefit. James Clear, the author of *Atomic Habits*, writes on his blog, "[I]f you want to set your expectations appropriately, the truth is that it will probably take you anywhere from two months to eight months to build a new behavior into your life—not 21 days."[2]

Each of us is different and each section can require different demands from us. Therefore, whatever date you set to work on a section, give yourself an initial "Targeted 8 to 10 Scale Date" at ninety days out. This number falls in the range provided by James Clear. As you work your sections, things like distractions can be harder to recognize, track, record, and measure. You'll need time to realize when it impacts your time and reflect on the changes you need to make to improve.

Let me remind you not to work on a lot of categories and their sections at one time. Start with *Personal Care* and move down, trying not to implement more than three sections at a time (lead with one and see what happens).

How about we walk through one together? Procrastination is a challenge for many, so let's practice with that.

Category	Section	Start Date	Targeted 8 to 10 Scale Date	Actual 8 to 10 Scale Date
	Procrastination	2/13	5/14	
Internal Focus	Distractions			
	Motivation			

FIGURE 10:8 EXAMPLE FOR SETTING UP PROCRASTINATION

This time-optimized activity will be in addition to your current schedule, projects, and tasks. Your procrastination endeavor requires you to critically evaluate what you do right now. Therefore, the steps might look like something in Figure 10:9.

Process	Activity	Action
Step 1	Create main task—Overcoming Procrastination	This will be the "master" or "mission" statement to accomplish. Maybe title it, "Overcoming Procrastination." Set complete date at 5/14.
Step 2	Subtask 1—Daily Procrastination Check	Make a daily recurring subtask (end date 5/14) to remind you toward the end of the workday by asking, "Are there any tasks I did not get done because I procrastinated?" If the answer is yes, determine what changes need to take place.
Step 3	Subtask 2—Weekly Procrastination Check	Create an end-of-week reoccurring task to dive deep into the current week and evaluate your activity for the next week to identify and address any current and potential procrastination items. Ask yourself, "On a scale of 1 (novice) to 10 (expert), how well am I handling procrastination?" Establish an end date of 5/14.
Step 4	Calendar—Procrastination Dedication Meeting	Generate a weekly (reoccurring) event on your calendar. Try to establish it as protected time. Review and evaluate your current progress.

FIGURE 10:9 A PROCRASTINATION EXECUTION EXAMPLE

In essence, Figure 10:9 is an extreme simplification of what we discussed back in Chapter 4. As with all sections you identify as time-optimized opportunities, review their areas in the book before implementing. You'll notice as well that the approach used is narrow and specific. There is one primary task, two subtasks, and a dedicated event/meeting. Use "Priority Category Execution" as a check on your current activities, not a disruption of your entire way of doing things. You'll notice that as you highlight or place emphasis on a section like procrastination, other areas will naturally improve over time. You may even find you solve lower-level problem areas even before you choose to work on them.

Finally, the end date is a goal. After eight weeks, you should answer, "I am an 8 on the 1–10 scale," then move to the next section. You don't need to stay if it is not a challenge. Conversely, if it takes longer, do not punish yourself. Set a new date and keep working. Hark back to our eight-month habit length.

There is a chance for backsliding, seeming to have solved a time-optimized process, only to have it come back. No worries. Just set up and execute again. I have had to do this multiple times as I constantly battle distractions.

SELF-SELECTING AND POTPOURRI: EXECUTION

In case you jumped right to this part because you identify as a Self-Selecting or Potpourri person, I am going to make you go back because, at some point, I reference items that are discussed in "Priority Category Execution" that will be used here as well.

When last we left you in the preparation phase, you had completed self-selecting the sections for improvement in Figure 10:5. Depending on your current time optimization comfort, you either identified full categories of attention (self-selecting), or you only had the need to pick and choose the sections that stood out for some tender-loving care (potpourri). Like shown in Figure 10:7, you now need to establish your time-optimized timelines. Only, unlike that chart, you'll need to fill in the categories and sections based on the calculations done in Figure 10:5 by using the table below.

Category	Section	Current 1 to 10 Rating	Start Date	Targeted 8 to 10 Scale Date	Actual 8 to 10 Scale Date

Category	Section	Current 1 to 10 Rating	Start Date	Targeted 8 to 10 Scale Date	Actual 8 to 10 Scale Date

FIGURE 10:10 ESTABLISHING RANKING AND TIME-OPTIMIZED TIMELINES

I recommend you fill the entire chart out, even if you gave yourself a lot of high scores. Time optimization is not like riding a bike. Once you get comfortable, you can then forget and lose your balance and need to relearn (for example: yours truly and distractions). It is dedication to keep at it that can make the process effortless.

For the Self-Selecting folks, you will rank your categories first (the lowest average score) and then sort the sections within each category. If you are a Potpourri, simply rank your sections from lowest to highest in the third column. You are choosing not to emphasize a particular category.

You may be thinking, "Well, that is a waste of time from the guy who keeps preaching about saving time to fill out everything." I have a solution for you, head on over to the Resources section and find the information to take the Time Management Analysis, where all of this is done for you. Ultimately, you have free will; do what works best for your level.

Once you have your distinctive execution plan in place, fill in the start date for each section. As noted in the previous segment, less is more. Any section you execute already layers on top of your life.

Repeating what was introduced in the last section, based on the timing needed for a new activity to become a habit, set your targeted completion date at ninety days—and only when you are ready to execute. Otherwise, keep the date blank. Once you feel comfortable rating yourself between eight and ten (even if it is before the due date), move to the next category or section on the list. Need more time? Do not punish yourself; pick a new date and keep at it.

If you need an example to provide inspiration, check out Figure 10:9, which shows a situation to overcome procrastination. See, I mentioned you would need to go back.

STRATEGY: CONTROL

"Strategy Control," like so many other elements of control in this book, is direct and specific. You want to quickly ascertain if you have prepared well and are executing efficiently. That can easily be done with a series of simple questions.

- Am I working too many sections at a time?
- Have I set my tasks correctly?
- Am I working on those tasks and completing them on time?
- Have I allocated dedicated time to focus on my opportunity?
- Am I using my reserved time to help make progress?
- Do I feel like I am improving?
- Will I make my target date?

Answering no to one or more of the questions does not mean you are a failure. Do not give up! PEC is a continuous process, refining your approach until your skill is sharpened. You might be experiencing an entirely new way of looking at your use of time. It is not out of the question to think it may take you a few iterations to move forward in a way that is right for your circumstances. Let "Strategy Control" be positive correction and guidance.

While the control questions you ask search for the "no" in your section strategy, there is an additional question that ponders action when the answer is "yes."

- Do I need help?

Please, do not think you have to go this alone. You are surrounded by time-optimized specialists in your life. Seek them out as mentors.

TIME-OPTIMIZED MENTOR (TOM)

Each of the people I featured in Chapters 3 through 8 is like a next-door neighbor, friend, or coworker in your life today. Unlike Jeff Bezos and Elon Musk, the time-optimized individuals are relatable.

Think about it; in your life today, you know a good planner like Tracy Holmes. In your orbit is a Matt Anselmo, who is a solid task administrator. Your network has an internally focused individual along the lines of Hunter Camp. At hand is access to a Divya Jaitly, who will set an example of external focus. In your family, there is bound to be a great organizer like Ellie Buck. When it comes to personal care, a Julie Blacutt awaits.

Seek out those who lead by example and glean as much information as possible. Tell them what you are trying to accomplish and ask for their assistance. Let them hold you accountable. Unlike traditional mentors (which tend to develop organically and can last a lifetime), a time-optimized mentor is narrow and focused. A TOM is:

- Designed to help you improve in a specific category and even a single section.
- Meant to be used for a limited time, until you self-rate at an eight or above.
- There to provide an example of what to do right.
- There to encourage and not handhold.

You may choose to use the same person as your TOM in multiple areas. Just be careful. You do not want to copy their style but improve and adapt your time from managing to optimizing. Using different people brings diverse perspectives and ideas. The people you read about in the book range in age from their twenties to their sixties. They live in different parts of the United States and India. You don't need to go that wide; time-optimized people are everywhere.

THE ONE THING

"What is the one thing you would recommend I work on when it comes to my time management?"

I get asked this question a lot. I do not like to answer. Time optimization is different for each of us. Should I say, "interruptions" . . . well, then anyone who manages that well might think they are set and will be robbed of the productivity opportunities represented through the time-optimized journey.

However, if a million dollars were placed in front of me, and getting that money was contingent on me answering the question, I would answer. "The one thing I would recommend is to fully utilize your calendar and task programs so they are integrated into one powerful, time-optimized resource." There you have it: $1,000,000 worth of advice.

I have spoken a lot about each instrument in this book. The calendar and task list are readily available and well over 90 percent of people have access to them right now. For the rest of you, they are a free download away. Every topic we discussed in this book can be tied into the use of either tool. When you PEC the calendar and task list, executing time optimization is so much more efficient.

THE TIME-OPTIMIZED LIFE RECAP

I am so honored to have you come along on this time-optimized expedition. We started by looking at the view of time itself. Depending on your worldview, time can be seen as linear, cyclical, or even illusionary. The application of PEC (preparation, execution, and control) applies all aspects of those worldviews into a system of ever-increasing productivity. Time optimization seeks perfection, knowing it will never be attained, but the very effort itself brings a higher quality and fuller life.

Looking at time to be "managed" is reactive and static. Optimizing time changes the mindset to a proactive stance, always pursuing dynamic methods to bring meaning and purpose. The outcome is not to take away the joys in life. Contrary to that, a well-structured existence allows for powerful instances of spontaneous activity because time optimization permits an easy understanding of what needs to change in the future to account for an unstructured event.

One of the main aspects I fear about my life is maintaining a defined purpose. I suppose that is why I am drawn to the Scripture passage at the beginning of the chapter. It speaks to the timing of starting and stopping. What is beneficial now may not be later. The Book of Ecclesiastes was not written as a cheerful self-help guide to make you feel good or warm and fuzzy inside. It is populated by melancholy phrases.

"Utterly meaningless! Everything is meaningless" (Ecclesiastes 1:2).

"Better one handful with tranquility than two handfuls with toil and chasing after the wind" (Ecclesiastes 4:6).

To me, the book speaks of a busy life void of worth.

I have had many people I know pass away (as you get older, it becomes more of a reality). There have been myriad reasons, usually related to health ailments. However, in some cases, buried below the surface, you uncover the decline in the quality of life that started when there was an absence of meaning. The latter days became a repeating routine, lacking depth and substance. Time optimization is designed to fill the increased scheduled openings on the calendar with reason, intention, and hope.

On the other side, many of you are in the opposite situation. There are not enough hours in the day for you to get everything done. You wonder if sacrificing another sixty minutes of sleep will get more stuff completed. Time optimization is beneficial to bring the right allocation of time and refine your purpose to something more focused and meaningful.

Whether you dive into PEC with abandon, close the cover thinking of a way to regift this book, or fall somewhere in between, I want you to have a time-optimized life. One that is filled with time richness because you are continuously pursuing the finest in preparation, always precise in your execution, and gaining heightened control over your productivity.

Resources

Writing a book is not an easy undertaking. Thinking that people will then pick it up and read it is humbling. In appreciation of your efforts, the following are links to free resources that align with the content of this book. Please use and download them to assist you on your journey of the right *preparation* and the right *execution* that escalates broad *control* over your personal productivity.

TIME MANAGEMENT ANALYSIS (TMA)

This report provides an individual assessment of how you manage your time. It is the outline from which this book was created. The link below gives you access to the page specifically created for the readers of this book. Fill out the form and get your detailed assessment back within forty-eight hours. A $39.00 value, the TMA is free to you for purchasing The Time-Optimized Life.

www.infinitylifestyledesign.com/tma-book

LIFE PURPOSE STATEMENT (LPS)

In Chapter 3, we discussed the importance of setting goals. I mentioned my passion for helping people establish a life purpose statement. Enter the address below and download the Life Purpose Statement template to create a meaningful vision of what you can accomplish in your life.

www.infinitylifestyledesign.com/life-purpose

RETIREMENT TIME ANALYSIS (RTA)

For those getting close to retirement, the RTA report provides an individual assessment tied to your attitude and feelings about heading into a post-career life. The link below gives you access to the page specifically created for the readers of this book. Fill out the form and get your detailed assessment back within forty-eight hours. A $39.00 value, the RTA is also free to you for purchasing The Time-Optimized Life.

www.infinitylifestyledesign.com/rta-book

About the Authors

David Buck has amassed thirty-plus years of organizational and time management experience. That led him to start Kairos Management Solutions and the Infinity Lifestyle design program. Dave guides business professionals, who struggle with a lack of flexibility in their life and want more quality personal time. He helps his clients craft a strategy around their current management of time, that then defines a lifestyle focused on intention, ease, and joy. Dave resides in Ponte Vedra, Florida with his wife the Rev. Dr. Susan Rose.

Rev. Dr. Susan Rose is an ordained PC (USA) minister, a certified Spiritual Director, and the founder of Diakonos Solutions, a nonprofit dedicated to mentoring women in ministry. Susan lives what she calls "the hyphenated life"- incorporating part-time work and school, along with volunteer leadership into a busy family life. She published her dissertation Not-Quite-Equal: Mentoring Women for 21st Century Leadership in 2021 and has written articles for *The Presbyterian Outlook*. She understands the pressures of women managing work, family, and life goals. Susan lives in Ponte Vedra, Florida, with her husband, David Buck.

Endnotes

CHAPTER I: WHAT IS TIME OPTIMIZATION?

1. Amber Parion, "Calendars Used Around The World," https://www.worldatlas.com/articles/calendars-used-around-the-world.html, (accessed September 4, 2022).

2. Wayne Jackson, "The Biblical Concept of Time," https://www.christiancourier.com/articles/437-the-biblical-concept-of-time, (accessed September 4, 2022).

3. Tzvi Freeman, "What Is Time?" https://www.chabad.org/library/article_cdo/aid/74335/jewish/What-Is-Time.htm, (accessed September 4, 2022).

4. Arisha Stacey, "The Value of Time," https://www.islamreligion.com/articles/4155/value-of-time/, (accessed September 2, 2022).

5. "Time in Hinduism," https://www.hinduamerican.org/wp-content/uploads/2019/12/TimeinHinduism2.00_1-2.pdf, (accessed September 2, 2022).

6. Barbara O'Brien, "About Time from A Buddhist Perspective," https://www.learnreligions.com/about-time-449562 (accessed September 5, 2022).

7. Lee Smolin, "Temporal naturalism," https://www.sciencedirect.com/science/article/abs/pii/S1355219815000271, (accessed September 2, 2022).

8. *The Autobiography of Benjamin Franklin*, https://www.ushistory.org/franklin/autobiography/page38.htm#:~:text=Lose%20no%20time%3B%20be%20always,if%20you%20speak%2C%20speak%20accordingly.&text=Wrong%20none%20by%20doing%20injuries,benefits%20that%20are%20your%20duty (accessed September 2, 2022).

9. "Benjamin Franklin's Famous Quotes," https://www.fi.edu/benjamin-franklin/famous-quotes, (accessed September 2, 2022).

10. "Time Management: A Definition," https://www.glassdoor.com/blog/guide/time-management-definition/, (accessed September 11, 2022).

11. Brigadier Sushil Bhasin, *Million Dollar Second*, (Mumbi: TV18 Broadcast Ltd, 2019), p. 34.

12. Cal Newport, *Deep Work* (New York: Grand Central Publishing, 2016), p. 222.

13. Mark Crawford, "5 Lean Principles Every Engineer Should Know," https://www.asme.org/topics-resources/content/5-lean-principles-every-should-know (accessed September 8, 2022).

14. Lean Enterprise Institute, "A Brief History of Lean," https://www.lean.org/explore-lean/a-brief-history-of-lean/ (accessed September 11, 2022).

CHAPTER 2: THE FIVE AREAS OF OPTIMIZATION

1. Courtney Hayes, "Inside Jeff Bezos Daily Routine", https://www.youtube.com/watch?v=upB7ORf6o8Q (accessed September 6, 2022).

2. Finty Team, "Jeff Bezos daily routine", https://finty.com/us/daily-routines/jeff-bezos/#:~:text=His%20most%20productive%20time%20is,day's%20priority%20meetings%20and%20paperwork (accessed September 6, 2022).

3. Ibid

4. Hao, "Elon Musk: Daily Routine", https://balancethegrind.co/daily-routines/elon-musk-daily-routine/ (accessed September 6, 2022).

5. Chaitra Anand, "Elon Musk's 5 everyday habits that make him successful", https://ph.news.yahoo.com/elon-musks-5-everyday-habits-that-keep-him-successful-102831595.html (accessed September 6, 2022).

6. Áine Cain and Taylor Nicole Rogers, "A look at the demanding schedule of Elon Musk, who plans his day in 5-minute slots, constantly multitasks, and avoids phone calls", https://www.businessinsider.com/elon-musk-daily-schedule-2017-6 (accessed September 7, 2022).

7. Howe Q. Wallace, "The Five P's: 'Proper Preparation Prevents Poor Performance'", https://www.hqnotes.com/the-five-ps-proper-preparation-prevents-poor-performance/, (accessed September 12, 2022).

8. The NIV Study Bible, (Grand Rapids: Zondervan Publishing House, 1995), p. 1,566.

9. Dom Galeon, "Here's a List of Everything Elon Musk Says He'll Do by 2030," https://futurism.com/heres-list-everything-elon-musk-2030, (accessed September 13, 2022).

10. Sean Wolfe, "Jeff Bezos says he complains to his staff . . ." https://www.businessinsider.com/jeff-bezos-forbes-interview-works-years-in-future-2018-9, (accessed September 13, 2022).

11. Christian Soschner, "This One Time Management Method Makes Elon Musk the Most Successful Entrepreneur", https://medium.datadriveninvestor.com/this-one-time-management-method-makes-elon-musk-the-most-successful-entrepreneur-1af5a0ad507a, (accessed September 13, 2022).

12. Justin Bariso, "Why Brilliant Minds Like Jeff Bezos Embrace the Simple Rule of Scope", https://www.inc.com/justin-bariso/why-brilliant-minds-like-jeff-bezos-embrace-simple-rule-of-scope.html, (accessed September 13, 2022).

13. "Quotes by Yogi Berra", https://best-quotations.com/authquotes.php?auth=1018, (accessed September 14, 2022).

14. Mark Ritson, "Jeff Bezos's success at Amazon is down to one thing: focusing on the customer https://www.marketingweek.com/mark-ritson-jeff-bezos-success-focusing-on-customer/, (accessed September 16, 2022).

15. Catherine Clifford, "Here's Elon Musk's morning routine—and his top productivity tip", https://www.cnbc.com/2017/06/20/elon-musks-morning-routine-and-top-productivity-tip.html, (accessed September 16, 2022).

16. Liana Dagdevirenel , "Elon Musk's Time Management Technique: Time-boxing", https://medium.com/insumo/elon-musks-time-management-technique-timeboxing-2f30021a4863, (accessed September 16, 2022).

17. Catherine Clifford, "Jeff Bezos: This is how I organize my time," https://www.yahoo.com/lifestyle/jeff-bezos-organize-time-183417438.html, (accessed September 16, 2022).

18. Sreeraj M Ajay, "Jeff Bezos' Daily Routine, Workout & Diet," https://www.drworkout.fitness/jeff-bezos-daily-routine/, (accessed September 16, 2022).

19. The House of Routine, "5 Things You Can Learn From Elon Musk's Daily Routine", https://thehouseofroutine.com/blogs/news/5-things-you-can-learn-from-elon-musk-s-daily-routine, (accessed September, 16 2022).

20. Georgetown University Center for Child and Human Development, "Definitions and Discussion of Spirituality and Religion", https://nccc.georgetown.edu/body-mind-spirit/definitions-spirituality-religion.php, (accessed October 15, 2022).

21. The NIV Study Bible, p. 1,893.

CHAPTER 3: TIME-OPTIMIZED PLANNING

1. Reclaim.ai Blog, "Productivity Trends Report: One-on-One Meeting Statistics", https://reclaim.ai/blog/productivity-report-one-on-one-meetings#:~:text=Professionals%20average%2021.5%20hours%20in,14.2%20hours%20in%20weekly%20meetings, (accessed September 18, 2022).

2. YouVersion, NIV Bible translation, https://www.bible.com/search/bible?query=2%20timothy%204%3A2-12, (accessed May 10, 2023).

3. The website of Tracy and Rhonda Holmes, https://theworddietbook.com/.

4. Michael Hyatt and Daniel Harkavy, *Living Forward*, (Grand Rapids, Baker Publishing Group, 2016).

5. Ben Zimmer, "The Origins of 'Bucket List'," https://www.wsj.com/articles/the-origins-of-bucket-list-1432909572, (accessed September 21, 2022).

6. David Allen, *Getting Things Done*, (London, Piatkus, 2015), p.60.

7. Roger Connors, Tom Smith, and Craig Hickman, *The Oz Principle*, (New York, Penguin Group, 2004), p. 191.

8. Julie Nguyen, "How Many Goals Should I Set At Once?" https://www.habitify.me/blog/how-many-goals-should-i-set, (accessed September 21,2022).

9. UAB Medicine Marketing, "10 Secrets of People Who Keep Their New Year's Resolutions", https://www.uabmedicine.org/-/10-secrets-of-people-who-keep-their-new-year-s-resolutions#:~:text=Less%20than%208%25%20of%20people,about%20sticking%20to%20your%20goals., (accessed September 23 ,2022).

10. Discover Daily Habits, "New Year's Resolution Statistics (2022 Updated)", https://discoverhappyhabits.com/new-years-resolution-statistics/#2019-statistics, (accessed September 23 ,2022).

11. T. Rowe Price, "Three Themes Shaping the U.S Retirement Landscape in 2023," https://www.troweprice.com/content/dam/retirement-plan-services/pdfs/insights/retirement-market-outlook/Retirement_Market_Outlook_FullArticle.pdf, (accessed May 10, 2023).

12. Maria G. Hoffman, Mark A. Klee and Briana Sullivan, "New Data Reveal Inequality in Retirement Account Ownership," https://www.census.gov/library/stories/2022/08/who-has-retirement-accounts.html, (accessed September 23 ,2022).

13. Newsdesk, "Stats: Less Than Half of Americans Take Time to Plan Vacation Days", https://www.travelagentcentral.com/running-your-business/stats-less-than-half-americans-take-time-to-plan-vacation-days, (accessed September 23, 2022).

14. Ben Laker, Vijay Pereira, Ashish Malik, and Lebene Soga, "Dear Manager, You're Holding Too Many Meetings", https://hbr.org/2022/03/

dear-manager-youre-holding-too-many-meetings#:~:text=Our%20
research%20shows%20that%2092,a%20big%20contributor%20
to%20technostress., (accessed September 23 ,2022).

15. Patrick Lencioni, *Death by Meeting: A Leadership Fable*, (United States, HB Printing, 2004).

16. Ibid, p. 221–254.

17. *The Table Group*, https://www.tablegroup.com.

18. Matt Martin, "The State of Meetings in 2020", https://bettermeetings. expert/meeting-statistics/, (accessed September 25, 2022).

19. Jack Flynn, "28 Incredible Meeting Statistics [2022]," https://www. zippia.com/advice/meeting-statistics/#:~:text=The%20average%20 employee%20participates%20in,least%2012%20meetings%20per%20 week, (accessed September 25, 2022).

20. Charles Duhigg, *The Power of Habit*, (New York, Random House Trade Paperbacks, 2014), p. 270.

CHAPTER 4: TIME-OPTIMIZED TASK DESIGN

1. YouVersion, NIV Bible translation, https://www.bible.com/search/ bible?query=proverbs%2017%3A17, (accessed May 5, 2023).

2. Belle Beth Cooper, "The Surprising History of the To-Do List and How to Design One That Actually Works," https://buffer.com/resources/ the-origin-of-the-to-do-list-and-how-to-design-one-that-works/#:~: text=Benjamin%20Franklin%2C%20the%20godfather%20of,his%20 progress%20on%20a%20chart., (accessed September 26, 2022).

3. FS Blog, "A Brief History of the To-Do List," https://fs.blog/history-of- the-to-do-list/, (accessed September 26, 2022).

4. FranklinPlanner, https://shop.franklinplanner.com/store/, (accessed September 26, 2022).

5. Microsoft Office, https://www.office.com/, (accessed September 26, 2022).

6. "How to use Google Tasks," https://support.google.com/tasks/ answer/7675772?hl=en&co=GENIE.Platform%3DDesktop, (accessed September 26, 2022).

7. *Full Focus Planner*, https://fullfocusstore.com/, (accessed September 26, 2022).

8. Oberlo, "Most Used Email Clients Worldwide", https://www.oberlo.com/statistics/most-used-email-clients, (accessed September 26, 2022).

9. Denise Fournier Ph.D., "The Only Way to Eat an Elephant," https://www.psychologytoday.com/us/blog/mindfully-present-fully-alive/201804/the-only-way-eat-elephant, (accessed September 27, 2022).

10. Dave Ramsey, *EntreLeadership* (New York: Howard Books, 2011), p.49.

11. Carey Nieuwhof, *At Your Best*, (Colorado Spring: WaterBrook), p.50.

12. Planner Talk, "Your Refresher Course: How To Use The FranklinPlanner System", https://blog.franklinplanner.com/your-refresher-course-how-to-use-the-franklinplanner-system/, (accessed September 30, 2022).

13. *Merriam-Webster Dictionary*, https://www.merriam-webster.com/dictionary/multitasking, (accessed October 2, 2022).

14. *Cambridge Dictionary*, https://dictionary.cambridge.org/us/dictionary/english/multitasking, (accessed October 2, 2022).

15. Jeff Comer Psy.D., "The Fallacy of Multitasking," https://www.psychologytoday.com/us/blog/beyond-stress-and-burnout/202203/the-fallacy-multitasking#:~:text=(2013)%20reported%20that%20people%20who,thing%20only%20at%20a%20time., (accessed October 2, 2022).

16. *Technopedia* definition for multitasking, as quoted from Dave Crenshaw, *The Myth of Multitasking*, (Coral Gables, FL: Mango Publishing Group, 2021), p. 41.

17. Health Essentials, "Why Multitasking Doesn't Work", https://health.clevelandclinic.org/science-clear-multitasking-doesnt-work/#:~:text=Multitasking%20can%20hinder%20your%20performance,likely%20to%20make%20a%20mistake, (accessed October 2, 2022).

18. Peter Bregman, "How (and Why) to Stop Multitasking," https://hbr.org/2010/05/how-and-why-to-stop-multitaski, (accessed October 2, 2022).

19. Carey Lohrenz, "The Shocking Truth About Multitasking In The Age Of Distraction," https://www.forbes.com/sites/

forbesbooksauthors/2021/06/15/multitasking-in-the-age-of-distraction/?sh=39cb15334918, (accessed October 9, 2022).

CHAPTER 5: TIME-OPTIMIZED INTERNAL FOCUS

1. Lewis, N. A., & Oyserman, D.," Better Get to Work: Procrastination May Harm Heart Health", https://www.psychologicalscience.org/news/minds-business/better-get-to-work-procrastination-may-harm-heart-health.html, (accessed October 5, 2022).
2. Brian Tracy, *Eat that Frog*, (Oakland, CA, Berrett-Koehler, 2017), p.56.
3. Charlotte Lieberman, "Why You Procrastinate (It Has Nothing to Do With Self-Control)," https://www.nytimes.com/2019/03/25/smarter-living/why-you-procrastinate-it-has-nothing-to-do-with-self-control.html, (accessed October 5, 2022).
4. Sara Berg, MS, "What doctors wish patients knew about decision fatigue," https://www.ama-assn.org/delivering-care/public-health/what-doctors-wish-patients-knew-about-decision-fatigue, (accessed October 5, 2022).
5. Cindy Lamothe, "Understanding Decision Fatigue," https://www.healthline.com/health/decision-fatigue, (accessed October 5, 2022).
6. Michal Feyoh, "The 18 Top Motivational Speakers in the World for 2022," https://www.developgoodhabits.com/motivational-speakers/, (accessed October 6, 2022).
7. Morgan Heindel, "6 Highly Effective Ways to Motivate Your Employees," https://www.hrforhealth.com/blog/6-ways-to-motivate-your-healthcare-employees, (accessed October 6, 2022).
8. *Eat that Frog*, (Oakland, CA, Berrett-Koehler, 2017), p.68.
9. *Deep Work*, p. 157.

CHAPTER 6: TIME-OPTIMIZED EXTERNAL FOCUS

1. The NIV Study Bible, p. 1,893.
2. University of Exeter, "Office small talk has a big impact on employees' wellbeing, study finds," https://phys.org/news/2020-06-office-small-big-impact-employees.html, (accessed October 17, 2022).

3. Kate McFarlin, "How to Keep Talking at Work to a Minimum," https://smallbusiness.chron.com/keep-talking-work-minimum-10966.html, (accessed October 17, 2022).

4. *Death by Meeting: A Leadership Fable*, p. 236.

5. Timothy Ferriss, *The 4-Hour Work Week*, (New York, Harmony Books, 2010), p. 112.

6. UC Berkley, "The Impact of Interruptions," https://hr.berkeley.edu/impact-interruptions, (accessed October 21, 2022).

7. F. Diane Barth, "Why Is It Hard to Say 'No' and How Can You Get Better at It?" https://www.psychologytoday.com/us/blog/the-couch/201601/why-is-it-hard-say-no-and-how-can-you-get-better-it, (accessed October 23, 2022).

8. Stephen R. Cover, *The 7 Habits of Highly Effective People*, (New York, NY, Simon and Schuster, 2020), p. 178.

9. Ibid, p. 179.

10. Jonathan Alpert, Psychotherapist, "7 Tips for Saying No Effectively," https://www.inc.com/jonathan-alpert/7-ways-to-say-no-to-someone-and-not-feel-bad-about-it.html, (accessed October 25, 2022).

11. Jennifer Herrity, "How To Nicely Say 'No' (With 50 Examples)," https://www.indeed.com/career-advice/career-development/how-to-nicely-say-no , (accessed October 25, 2022).

CHAPTER 7: TIME-OPTIMIZED ORGANIZATION

1. Adam Toren, "See It Through: 5 Steps to Finishing What You Start," https://www.entrepreneur.com/living/see-it-through-5-steps-to-finishing-what-you-start/235820, (accessed October 27, 2022).

2. David Allen, *Getting Things Done*, p. 146.

3. Mallika Mitra, Scientists Have Pinpointed the Most Productive Time of the Day, and it's Not the Crack of Dawn," https://money.com/most-productive-time-of-day/, (accessed November 01, 2022).

4. YEC Council Post, "Three Ways To Use Time Blocking For Better Time Management," https://www.forbes.com/sites/theyec/2021/09/15/

three-ways-to-use-time-blocking-for-better-time-management/?sh= 2f1d27af37f9, (accessed November 2, 2022).

5. *The Big Bang Theory* website, "Sheldon Cooper,," https://the-big-bang-theory.com/characters.Sheldon/, (accessed November 2, 2022).

6. Monk Wiki, "Adrain Monk," https://monk.fandom.com/wiki/Monk_ (TV_series), (accessed November 2, 2022).

7. Meineke.com, "Wheel Lug Nuts Bolts," https://www.meineke.com/ dictionary/wheel-lug-nuts-bolts/, (accessed November 2, 2022).

CHAPTER 8: TIME-OPTIMIZED PERSONAL CARE

1. Division of Sleep Medicine at Harvard Medical School, "Benefits of Sleep," https://healthysleep.med.harvard.edu/healthy/matters/ benefits-of-sleep, (accessed November 4, 2022).

2. "Getting Enough Sleep?" https://www.cdc.gov/sleep/features/getting-enough-sleep.html, (accessed November 4, 2022).

3. "Oversleeping: Bad for Your Health?" https://www.hopkinsmedicine. org/health/wellness-and-prevention/oversleeping-bad-for-your-health, (accessed November 4, 2022).

4. Tim Newman, "Medical myths: How much sleep do we need?" https:// www.medicalnewstoday.com/articles/medical-myths-how-much-sleep-do-we-need, (accessed November 4, 2022).

5. Max Hirshkowitz, PhD, Kaitlyn Whiton, MHS, Steven M. Albert, PhD, Cathy Alessi, MD, Oliviero Bruni, MD, Lydia DonCarlos, PhD, Nancy Hazen, PhD, John Herman, PhD, Eliot S. Katz, MD, Leila Kheirandish-Gozal, MD, MSc, David N. Neubauer, MD, Anne E. O'Donnell, MD, Maurice Ohayon, MD, DSc, PhD, John Peever, PhD, Robert Rawding, PhD, Ramesh C. Sachdeva, MD, PhD, JD, Belinda Setters, MD, Michael V. Vitiello, PhD, J. Catesby Ware, PhD, Paula J. Adams Hillard, MD, "National Sleep Foundation's sleep time duration recommendations: methodology and results summary," https://www.sleephealth journal.org/article/S2352-7218(15)00015-7/fulltext, (accessed November 4, 2022).

6. Jay Summer, "Eight Health Benefits of Sleep," https://www.sleepfoundation.org/how-sleep-works/benefits-of-sleep, (accessed November 4, 2022).

7. *Million Dollar Second*, p. 48.

8. Mayo Clinic Staff, "Napping: Do's and don'ts for healthy adults," https://www.mayoclinic.org/healthy-lifestyle/adult-health/in-depth/napping/art-20048319, (accessed November 4, 2022).

9. Ibid.

10. Alan Kohll, "New Study Shows Correlation Between Employee Engagement And The Long-Lost Lunch Break," https://www.forbes.com/sites/alankohll/2018/05/29/new-study-shows-correlation-between-employee-engagement-and-the-long-lost-lunch-break/?sh=3e5e16bb4efc, (accessed November 6 2022).

11. Angela Grippo Ph.D., "Why and How You Should Take Breaks at Work," https://www.psychologytoday.com/us/blog/the-wide-wide-world-psychology/201704/why-and-how-you-should-take-breaks-work, (accessed November 6, 2022).

12. *Deep Work*, p.161.

13. Neil Patel, "When, How, and How Often to Take a Break," https://www.inc.com/neil-patel/when-how-and-how-often-to-take-a-break.html, (accessed November, 6, 2022).

14. *Deep Work*, p. 170.

15. Aaron Edelheit, *The Hard Break: The Case for a 24/6 Lifestyle*, (United States, Ideapress Publishing, 2018), p. 119.

16. CDC National Center for Health Statistics, "Exercise or Physical Activity," https://www.cdc.gov/nchs/fastats/exercise.htm, (accessed November 6, 2022).

17. Mayo Clinic Staff, "Exercise: 7 benefits of regular physical activity," https://www.mayoclinic.org/healthy-lifestyle/fitness/in-depth/exercise/art-20048389, (accessed November 6, 2022).

18. American College of Sports Medicine, "Trending Topic | Physical Activity Guidelines," https://www.acsm.org/education-resources/trending-topics-resources/physical-activity-guidelines, (accessed November 6, 2022).

19. Amanda Capritto, Giselle Castro-Sloboda, "When's the Best Time of Day to Exercise? We Settle the Debate With Science," https://www.cnet.com/health/fitness/whens-the-best-time-of-day-to-exercise/, (accessed November 6, 2022).

20. Better Health Channel, "Physical activity—staying motivated," https://www.betterhealth.vic.gov.au/health/healthyliving/physical-activity-staying-motivated, (accessed November 6, 2022).

21. Rev. Dr. Susan Rose, "Week 5: Gratitude," https://diakonossolutions.com/blog/f/week-5---gratitude, (accessed November 6, 2022).

CHAPTER 9: SUSAN ROSE, ANOTHER TIME-OPTIMIZED PERSPECTIVE

1. Megan Brenan, "Women Still Handle Main Household Tasks in U.S.," https://news.gallup.com/poll/283979/women-handle-main-household-tasks.aspx#:~:text=Story%20Highlights%201%20Women%20mainly%20responsible%20for%20laundry,does%20certain%20household%20tasks%20differ%20sharply%20by%20gender, (accessed May 25, 2023).

2. Leah Ruppanner, "Women aren't better multitaskers than men—they're just doing more work," https://theconversation.com/women-arent-better-multitaskers-than-men-theyre-just-doing-more-work-121620, (accessed May 25, 2023).

3. Ibid

4. Andee Tagle, "Changing the gender imbalance in housework may start with how we understand time," https://www.npr.org/2022/10/09/1127744337/changing-the-gender-imbalance-in-housework-may-start-with-how-we-understand-time, (accessed May 25, 2023).

5. Salene M. W. Jones, Ph.D., "Understanding and Overcoming All-or-Nothing Thinking," https://www.psychologytoday.com/us/blog/all-about-cognitive-and-behavior-therapy/202210/understanding-and-overcoming-all-or-nothing (accessed May 25, 2023). Another article, Ashley Carucci, "What Is All-or-Nothing Thinking and Why

It's Important to Manage It," https://psychcentral.com/health/all-or-nothing-thinking-examples, (accessed May 25, 2023).

CHAPTER 10: THE TIME-OPTIMIZED LIFE

1. Charles Duhigg, *The Power of Habit,* (United States, Random House Trade Paperbacks, 2014), p 17–18.
2. James Clear, "How Long Does it Actually Take to Form a New Habit? (Backed by Science)," https://jamesclear.com/new-habit#:~:text=On%20 average%2C%20it%20takes%20more,to%20form%20a%20new%20 habit., (accessed November 13, 2022).

A free ebook edition is available with the purchase of this book.

To claim your free ebook edition:

1. Visit MorganJamesBOGO.com
2. Sign your name CLEARLY in the space
3. Complete the form and submit a photo of the entire copyright page
4. You or your friend can download the ebook to your preferred device

Morgan James
BOGO™

A **FREE** ebook edition is available for you or a friend with the purchase of this print book.

CLEARLY SIGN YOUR NAME ABOVE

Instructions to claim your free ebook edition:
1. Visit MorganJamesBOGO.com
2. Sign your name CLEARLY in the space above
3. Complete the form and submit a photo of this entire page
4. You or your friend can download the ebook to your preferred device

Print & Digital Together Forever.

Snap a photo

Free ebook

Read anywhere